THE HUGUENOT CONNECTION

ARCHIVES INTERNATIONALES D'HISTOIRE DES IDÉES

INTERNATIONAL ARCHIVES OF THE HISTORY OF IDEAS

125

R.M. GOLDEN

(editor)

THE HUGUENOT CONNECTION: THE EDICT OF NANTES, ITS REVOCATION, AND EARLY FRENCH MIGRATION TO SOUTH CAROLINA

THE HUGUENOT CONNECTION: THE EDICT OF NANTES, ITS REVOCATION, AND EARLY FRENCH MIGRATION TO SOUTH CAROLINA

Edited by

R.M. GOLDEN

1988

KLUWER ACADEMIC PUBLISHERS
DORDRECHT / BOSTON / LANCASTER

Distributors

for the United States and Canada: Kluwer Academic Publishers, 101 Philip Drive, Norwell, MA 02061, USA
for the UK and Ireland: Kluwer Academic Publishers, MTP Press Limited, Falcon House, Queen Square, Lancaster LA1 1RN, UK
for all other countries: Kluwer Academic Publishers Group, Distribution Center, P.O. Box 322, 3300 AH Dordrecht, The Netherlands

Library of Congress Cataloging in Publication Data

```
The Huguenot connection : the Edict of Nantes, its revocation, and
  early French migration to South Carolina / edited by Richard M.
  Golden.
        p.   cm. -- (International archives of the history of ideas ;
  125)
    Includes bibliographical references and index.
    ISBN 9024736455
    1. Edict of Nantes. 2. Huguenots--South Carolina. 3. French-
  -South Carolina. 4. Church and state--France--History--17th
  century. 5. France--Church history--17th century.  I. Golden,
  Richard M., 1947-   . II. Series: Archives internationales
  d'histoire des idées ; 125.
  BR845.H78 1988
  274.4'07--dc19                                         87-31061
                                                            CIP
```

ISBN 90-247-3645-5
ISBN 90-247-2433-3 (series)

PRINTED IN THE NETHERLANDS

Contents

Acknowledgements

I am delighted to thank the many organizations and people who helped in the preparation of this book and the lecture series that formed its basis. The Huguenot Society of South Carolina, The Huguenot Society of the Founders of Manakin in the Colony of Virginia, the Council for European Studies, Virginia Manning Moses, and the Clemson University Department of History and College of Liberal Arts gave generous contributions. In addition, funding in part was provided by the South Carolina Committee for the Humanities, an agency of the National Endowment for the Humanities. In Charleston, the following offered kind support: the Reverend Philip Bryant, Pastor of the French Protestant (Huguenot) Church, Martha Burns, John B. Dozier, Theodore B. Guerard, John Horlbeck, Dr. Jane Mahler, and deRosset Myers. I thank also John Allen, Mrs. John Inman Bell, Jr., Robert Bireley, Leland Cox, Jr., Jay Crawford, Gina Crawford, Leonard Greenspoon, Margaret Lamb, Sandra Piazza, and Robert Waller for their help. I have benefited from the close reading of parts of this book by Thomas Brennen, Georgia Cowart, Jack Censer, David Fisher, Elborg Forster, Robert Forster, Albert Hamscher, Elisabeth Joiner, Sharon Kettering, Joseph Klaits, Robert Kreiser, Jessica Kross, Gary McCollim, Don McKale, William Mouso, Robert Mulvany, Buford Norman, Denis Paz, Orest Ranum, John Romeiser, Lois Shell, Jo Anne Seeley, Timothy Tackett, John B. Wolf, and John Wunder. Jon Butler, Elisabeth Labrousse, and Nicola Sutherland were a delight to work with and I am especially grateful to them.

INTRODUCTION

Richard M. Golden

Possibly the most famous event in Louis XIV's long reign (1643-1715) was the Revocation of the Edict of Nantes, issued by the French king on 17 October 1685 and registered five days later by the *parlement* of Paris, a sovereign judicial institution having jurisdiction over approximately one-half of the kingdom. The Edict of Fontainebleau (the Revocation's technical name, derived from the palace southeast of Paris where Louis had signed the act) declared illegal the public profession of Calvinist Protestantism and led perhaps as many as 200,000 Huguenots,[1] as French Protestants were known, to flee their homeland. They did so despite royal decrees against emigration and the harsh punishment (prison for women, the galleys for men) awaiting those caught escaping.

The Revocation is a landmark in the checkered history of religious toleration (or intolerance); Huguenots, many Roman Catholics, and historians of all persuasions have heaped scorn on Louis XIV for withdrawing the Edict of Nantes, issued by his grandfather, Henry IV (1589-1610). King Henry had proclaimed the 1598 Edict to be both "perpetual" and "irrevocable." Although one absolutist king could not bind his successors and although "irrevocable" in the context of French law simply meant irrevocable until superseded by another edict, historians have accused Louis XIV of breaking faith with Henry IV and the Huguenots.[2] Louis did only what Henry probably would have done had he possessed the requisite power. The Huguenots themselves undoubtedly would have snuffed out Catholicism had they enjoyed the upper hand. But the rigorous penalties against would-be Huguenot refugees and Louis

---

[1] Estimates vary, but 200,000 is reasonable. A more accurate assessment will depend on further research. Elisabeth Labrousse, *"Une foi, une loi, un roi?" La Révocation de l'Édit de Nantes* (Paris and Geneva, 1985), 208. The derivation of "Huguenot" is established fairly well in Janet G. Gray, "The Origin of the Word Huguenot," *The Sixteenth Century Journal*, 14 (Fall, 1983): 349-59.

[2] Many historians still fail to understand the sense of "perpetual" and "irrevocable" in the Edict of Nantes. Some recent examples include René-Jacques Lovy, *La Révocation. Trois siècles de souffrances des protestants français sous l'ancien régime* (Champigny, 1985), 72; Robin D. Gwynn, *Huguenot Heritage. The History and Contribution of the Huguenots in Britain* (London, 1985), 22; G. A. Rothrock, *The Huguenots: A Biography of a Minority* (Chicago, 1979), 124. On the legal meaning of "perpetual" and "irrevocable," see Roland Mousnier, *The Institutions of France under the Absolute Monarchy, 1598-1789.* Vol. 2, *The Origins of State and Society* (Chicago, 1984), 237.

XIV's supposed reneging on Henry's Edict (which had, after all, signified the end of thirty-six years of civil wars) have earned the Revocation a terrible notoriety.

The French government used extremely brutal measures against the Huguenots even before the Revocation, including destroying their temples (churches), closing their graveyards, taking their children as young as seven years old from parents to be brought up as Catholics, and forbidding Protestants to engage in occupations other than agriculture and trade. Numerous acts issued against the Huguenots during Louis's reign make one despair, even after three centuries. Most infamous was the intermittent use of the *dragonnades* (so named after dragoons, mounted infantry with muskets and pikes), whereby troops were quartered in Huguenot households, especially in the south, the center of Huguenot strength. Seventeenth-century soldiers were the dregs of society; they were encouraged to treat their "hosts" roughly. Destruction of furniture, beatings, and rapes occurred; mass conversions resulted, often by entire towns at the rumor that the dragoons were approaching.

The three essays in this book were given as lectures in Charleston and Clemson, South Carolina, in the fall of 1985 to commemorate the Revocation. Why commemorate, one might ask, such atrocities and inhumanity? As the essays demonstrate, the Revocation was extremely significant—people seem to agree on that—but its history is more nuanced than many have been led to believe.[3] The long story of the Revocation, itself a byword for religious persecution, must be seen in the context of the sixteenth and seventeenth centuries. From that vantage point, as our three authors show, we must understand the motives and actions of all involved, resisting the temptation to judge them according to the values of our society, one that is vastly different in its values and one that praises conditions—such as religious toleration and political democracy—that were generally anathema to the seventeenth-century mind. By our standards, most of the actors in the Revocation drama, Roman Catholic and Huguenot alike, could be found wanting. Few seemed to have had the ability to empathize, to place themselves in others' shoes.

Do we commemorate the Revocation as extraordinary, an unusual example of religious intolerance in Western Civilization, an anomaly in the history of

---

[3] For an account of different historians' interpretations of the Revocation, see Jean Baubérot, "Préface," in Labrousse, "*Une foi, une loi, un roi?*" 9-21.

Christianity? Alas, no, for the Revocation belongs in the mainstream of our heritage; it reminds us that the normal state of affairs has been religious intolerance, an intolerance implying that persecution and cruelty have characterized human conduct over the past three thousand years, at the very least. The overwhelming majority of people throughout the centuries has detested religious as well as social and political dissidents; it is not surprising that the Revocation was the most popular and religious act of Louis XIV's reign.

True toleration, in the sense of separation of church and state, was inconceivable in sixteenth-century France.[4] Moderate Frenchmen, advocating the existence (if only temporary) of more than one religion, avoided using such words as *tolérance* or *tolérer*. These were negative terms, implying endurance, of suffering or death, for example. Society might tolerate a second religion only if absolutely necessary, just as one might be compelled to tolerate pain or death. Toleration as a positive term, as a principle that allows for the existence of a variety of practices and beliefs without outside interference or molestation, did not emerge until the eighteenth century with the Age of Enlightenment. Those who lived in France during the sixteenth-century wars of religion did not even possess the linguistic tools necessary for such a concept.[5] The idea of toleration, as we know it today, was completely foreign to them.

Political structures functioned to impose uniformity from above, in early modern France as indeed throughout Western Civilization. In religion, but in law, education, and in social matters as well, authority was to be accepted and revered, not questioned or divided. The child was to obey the parent, the wife her husband, the serf his lord, the subject his king, and every Christian the one, true Church. Very few before the modern era would question this pattern, based as it was on the assumption that all power descended from god and was modeled on god's plan.[6] Only a handful of exceptional individuals who rose beyond their culture pleaded for patience toward

---

[4] Bernard Dompnier, *Le venin de l'hérésie. Image du protestantisme et combat catholique au XVIIe siècle* (Paris, 1985), 25.

[5] William H. Huseman, "The Expression of the Idea of Toleration in French During the Sixteenth Century," *The Sixteenth Century Journal*, 15 (Fall, 1984): 293-310.

[6] I choose not to accept the conventional wisdom that capitalizes the Judeo-Christian "God." Such a capitalization implies a bias that is western and presentist and demeans other cultures' gods through the use of the lower case. In this matter I follow the arguments of Richard C. Trexler, "Reverence and Profanity in the Study of Early Modern Religion," in *Religion and Society in Early Modern Europe, 1500-1800*, ed. Kasper von Greyerz (London, 1984), 261-62.

the opinions of others. To be sure, there did appear from time to time small groups, islands of religious dissent in a sea of dogmatic uniformity, which necessarily had, for the sake of survival, to demand toleration. But these groups before the seventeenth century invariably failed the "power test." Did they, having called for toleration, grant it themselves after gaining power?[7]

We do not find doctrines of religious liberty embedded in the Old Testament, rigorous books that punish blasphemy with death and call for terrible vengeance against false prophets and idolators. Old Testament kingship became the model for a theocratic state, for there was no separation of church and state among the ancient Hebrews. The Old Testament had enormous influence on Christianity's subsequent intolerance toward other faiths. By linking heresy to blasphemy, medieval and Reformation Christians could with good conscience cast heretics to the flames, and Protestants defended their desecration of Catholic churches on grounds of idolatry. Christian kings, like their Old Testament predecessors, served as secular watchdogs of religious values. Throne upheld altar, both indissolubly linked against any unorthodox questioning of political and religious authority. It is not coincidental that when Christian churches have been persecuted they have laid the Old Testament aside, but when they have assumed power they have had greater recourse to the Hebrew scriptures.[8]

How far the Hebrews were from the lazy tolerance toward other gods and religions practiced by various other ancient peoples, such as the Egyptians and Mesopotamians! The god of the Hebrews called for the destruction of different cultures in Canaan, and the Hebrews relentlessly and brutally followed their god's pitiless instructions. Monotheism endowed its adherents with the knowledge that they alone were correct, that they alone knew the truth. Polytheistic societies, not always knowing the exact number of gods and conscious of the gods' sometimes fickle, even whimsical behavior, adjusted to the different beliefs of other societies. A pantheon of a hundred gods had room for a few more. Not until the Hebrews were

---

[7] Joseph Lecler, *Toleration and the Reformation*, 2 vols. (New York and London, 1960), 2:483.

[8] In my brief foray into the history of religious toleration, I have relied for the most part on Lecler, *Toleration and the Reformation*; Ian Haslett, "Scripture, Tradition and Intolerance: An Introduction to the Critique of Sebastian Castellio (1515-1563)," *Irish Biblical Studies*, 6 (1984): 106-119; Henry Kamen, *The Rise of Toleration* (New York and Toronto, 1967).

conquered, dispersed, and persecuted did they discover the virtue of religious toleration.

The New Testament, written between 60 and 110 A.D. when Christianity was a minority religion, contains passages that can be interpreted to support religious freedom. In Matthew 22:21, Jesus advised the Pharisees to "Render therefore to Caesar the things that are Caesar's, and to God the things that are God's." This is astute; a minority religion does well to argue that the government be accorded its just due. Nevertheless, separation of church and state is implicit in the statement attributed to Jesus. Furthermore, aside from expelling the money changers from the temple, Jesus counseled against violence. For him and his disciples, verbal persuasion and teaching by example were to be the only means employed to win converts. Paul argued that Christian charity required respect for another's conscience (1 Corinthians 10:28-29).

In the face of sporadic repression by the Roman government, which normally accepted religious diversity,[9] Christianity urged toleration. Early theologians praised liberty of conscience during the first three centuries. This position did not preclude quarrels among Christian groups, as Gnostics, Donatists, Monophysites, Nestorians, and Arians—to mention a few—contested bitterly for custody of the truth with the eventual winners, labeled now as orthodox Christians.

In the fourth century, when the Roman Empire became Christianized, Christians forgot their calls for liberty of conscience. The Edict of Constantinople of 392 outlawed paganism; another law, in 407, decreed the death penalty for heretics. We can see this development in Saint Augustine (354-430), Bishop of Hippo in North Africa and the greatest of the Latin Church Fathers. Augustine invoked the aid of the secular powers to crush the Donatists, and interpreted the parable of the supper (Luke 14:23)—whereby Jesus orders the servant to "go out to the highways and hedges, and compel people to come in, that my house may be filled"—as justification for compulsion. In the bestial words of Augustine, "The Church persecutes out of

---

[9] See M. de Ste Croix, "Why Were the Early Christians Persecuted?" in *Studies in Ancient Society,* ed. M. I. Finely (London, 1974), 210-49; and Peter Garnsey, "Toleration in Classical Antiquity," in *Persecution and Toleration,* ed. W. J. Shiels (London, 1984), 1-27.

love, the ungodly out of cruelty."[10] The religious totalitarianism of Louis XIV fed on seeds planted by Augustine.

For Europeans of the Middle Ages, order had god's blessing. Just as one god had created the universe, so should there exist only one Church headed by one individual, the Bishop of Rome. One king should govern one kingdom or, better yet according to medieval political theory, one Christian emperor should preside over Europe. Multiplicity was an abomination.

Reality was another matter. Feudal lords fought with one another and with their kings; kings fought with other kings and quarreled with popes. Beginning in the eleventh century with increased urbanization and a rise in population, heretical groups appeared. Towns and the new social group, the bourgeoisie, associated with them, proved fertile ground for the dissemination of ideas. Regions grew less isolated as merchants traveled, trade increased, and peasants migrated to urban centers. Since the eleventh century, the custom of burning heretics became more common. According to the great medieval theologian, Thomas Aquinas (1225-74), heresy was a disease that had to be cut out from the body politic. The Church practiced absolute intolerance toward those it deemed to be heretics.

On the other hand, the medieval Church, including Aquinas, offered relative toleration toward infidels, that is, Moslems and Jews. Although the crusaders going to recover the Holy Land slaughtered Moslems and while pogroms, widespread in the eleventh and fourteenth centuries, entailed the massacre of thousands of Jews, the Church hierarchy, for the most part, distinguished between non-Christians, somewhat protected by their "invincible ignorance," and apostates, heretics who had knowingly left the orthodox fold. Theologians could argue that force should not be used to convert pagans, but Christians could agree that compulsion was necessary to bring heretics back to the bosom of Holy Mother Church. Christianity since the end of the eleventh century battled the Moslems to the east. Could the Church successfully wage foreign war when traitors—heretics—gnawed at her from within?

---

[10] Kamen, *The Rise of Toleration*, 13-14.

Threats from outside and inside Europe gained in intensity by the time the Protestant Reformation occurred in the sixteenth century. The Ottoman Turks had finished their conquest of the Christian Byzantine Empire in 1453; now they moved up the Danube toward western Europe, subjugating the Balkans and Hungary before arriving at the gates of Vienna in 1683.[11] Christianity was under siege. Popes preached crusades, while one of the first uses of the printing press was to galvanize Europeans against the Turks. At the same time the Protestant Reformation, beginning in 1517, permanently rent the fabric of a relatively united medieval Christianity. The Roman Catholic Church now confronted a plethora of Protestant faiths, which fought among themselves even as they depicted the pope as the Antichrist.

Both Catholics and Protestants could agree that religious liberty was to be avoided. Although Martin Luther (1483-1546) preached the priesthood of all believers and argued that every man should be his own priest and read the Bible for himself, he was aghast when others interpreted the Bible differently. Luther feared social revolution and realized that those in power who supported him would not stand for any liberty. The establishment of Lutheran churches necessitated compulsion. On practical grounds, then, Luther had to abandon toleration. Indeed, he even went beyond the medieval Church in his intolerance. At first sanguine that Jews would see the light and convert in droves, he became viciously anti-Semitic after he realized that they would not accept his message: "I say to you lastly, as a countryman, if the Jews refuse to be converted, we ought not to suffer them or bear with them any longer."[12]

The other great Protestant reformer, John Calvin (1509-64), was no less intolerant than Luther. The city government of Geneva, the "Protestant Rome," executed, with Calvin's support, the Spaniard Michael Servetus (1511-53), who had denied the Christian doctrine of the Trinity. In the *Defence of the Orthodox Faith,* Calvin maintained: "We must resist the temptation to be influenced by feelings of humanity in these matters."[13]

---

[11] The Turks had previously reached Vienna in 1529 and western Hungary in 1532 and again in 1598.

[12] Cited in Abram Leon Sachar, *A History of the Jews* (New York, 1973), 229.

[13] Cited in Haslett, "Scripture, Tradition, and Intolerance," 114.

There was precious little humanity in matters of religious dispute during the sixteenth century. The Reformation was an era of religious wars or, rather, warfare among different faiths, for religion often simply provided a vehicle for other motivations, such as personal, economic, or political ambitions. In addition to the intermittent conflict against the Turks, war between Catholics and Protestants broke out in Germany in 1546. This struggle concluded temporarily in 1555 with the Peace of Augsburg, a settlement that, under the formula *cuius regio, eius religio* ("whose the region, his the religion"), allowed rulers in Germany to determine whether their states would be either Lutheran or Catholic. No other religions were acceptable alternatives and subjects had no choice whatsoever. (A similar arrangement providing for confessional parity existed among Swiss cantons.)[14] The Augsburg settlement proved ineffective and religious conflict in Germany did not cease until the Peace of Westphalia in 1648, which brought to a close the destructive Thirty Years' War. That war saw political and military attempts to roll back Protestantism in the Holy Roman Empire and so bring about that religious conformity so valued by the medieval Church and—let us not forget—by the Protestant reformers.

France struggled through civil and religious wars from 1562 to 1598. These conflicts were inextricably bound up with the international situation. Into France's troubled waters dived Catholic Spain, which made strenuous efforts to suppress the revolt of the Dutch, begun in 1566. The Duke of Alba (1507-82), Spanish governor-general and regent of the Netherlands, conducted a reign of terror in order to keep the southern provinces Catholic, while the northern provinces (Holland and Zealand) looked to France or England for support.

Under Elizabeth I (1558-1603), England experienced an ecumenical approach to the problem of religious difference. Although Elizabeth had claimed she did not want to make windows into men's souls, she intended to create a comprehensive religious settlement and so persecuted the contumacious, both Protestants and Catholics, who would not conform to her laws regarding religious behavior. In the latter part of Elizabeth's reign, Catholics were executed for treason and Protestants for

---

[14] Hans R. Guggisberg, "The Defence of Religious Toleration and Religious Liberty in Early Modern Europe: Arguments, Pressures, and Some Consequences," *History of European Ideas*, 4 (1983): 44-45.

radicalism.[15] Such was the English *via media*. As successful as Elizabeth were Portugal, Spain, and the Italian states, using their inquisitions—less bloodthirsty than previously thought—to protect their religious purity from Protestants, Moriscos, and Judaisers.[16]

Religious intolerance extended also to alleged witches, thought to have signed pacts with Satan to wreak evil on society. Protestants and Catholics could agree that witchcraft threatened to overturn Christianity, to turn the world upside down. The upshot was the execution of approximately one hundred thousand people, 80 percent of whom were women, for impossible activities. This European witch-craze, or mania, was part of the attempt by Protestants and resurgent Catholics to suppress elements of popular religiosity believed to conflict with the elite's new religious fervor.[17] The more the religious fervor, the greater the fanaticism and intolerance. Christian society was afraid of witches, of Turks, and of religious difference, to say nothing of revolts, plague, and famine.[18]

There were some in the sixteenth century who were prepared to endure different religious persuasions. Christian humanists such as Erasmus of Rotterdam (1466-1536) pleaded for toleration, but one that was temporary, leading eventually to Christian unity. Some mystics—the Germans Sebastian Franck (1499-1542) and Caspar Schwenckfeld (1489-1561), for example—argued for religious freedom because the only master of souls was the Holy Ghost. Minorities during the Reformation clamored for freedom of worship, but did not grant it to others when they became the majority religion. Among these may be included Lutherans, Anabaptists (who established a religious despotism in the German city of Münster), and English Puritans, some of whom migrated to New England. Only the seventeenth-century Baptists associated with Roger Williams (1603-83) in Rhode Island and with William Penn (1644-1718) and the Quakers in Pennsylvania were indulgent of the opinions of others. (There was, of course, the famous Maryland Toleration Act of 1649, but it ap-

[15] See David Lindsay Keir, *The Constitutional History of Modern Britain since 1485* (New York, 1967), 84-93.

[16] See William Monter, *Ritual, Myth and Magic in Early Modern Europe* (Athens, Ohio, 1984), 61-76.

[17] For an excellent overview of the witch-craze, see Joseph Klaits, *Servants of Satan: The Age of the Witch Hunts* (Bloomington, 1985).

[18] Jean Delumeau, *La peur en occident, XIVe-XVIIIe siècles* (Paris, 1978).

plied only to Trinitarians.) Furthermore, there were few, even among those who desired religious freedom, who would go so far as to tolerate atheists. Among those were Dirck Coornhert (1522-90), Roger Williams, and the Huguenot philosopher, Pierre Bayle (1647-1706). Even so outspoken an advocate for toleration as Sebastian Castellio (1515-63) did not deign to suffer atheists. Nevertheless, this Protestant saw clearly what was not apparent to most of his coreligionists in the sixteenth century. "To kill a man," he stated, "is not to defend a doctrine, but simply to kill a man."[19] The French Catholic humanist, Michel de Montaigne (1533-92), also chided the religious extremists: "After all, it is putting a very high price on one's conjectures to have a man roasted alive because of them."[20]

In sixteenth-century Europe, few states joined unity with religious division. Transylvania accepted in 1570 the legality of Catholicism, Lutheranism, Calvinism, and Unitarianism. In the Warsaw Confederation (1573), Poland placed a degree of religious liberty in the constitution, though only the aristocracy, which dominated the peasantry, benefited from this. The Dutch practiced toleration *de facto,* realizing that such a policy benefited the economy; their live and let live attitude may have influenced the 1598 religious settlement in France. The Edict of Nantes (see Appendix I) was the most famous example of the legal acceptance of confessional disunity.[21]

Henry IV had been in an unusual position for a king; since coming to the throne in 1589 he had had to carry on a war against Spain as well as fight those in France who denied that he was the legitimate king. His conversion (July 1593) failed to pacify extreme Catholics, while Protestants felt betrayed and so revived their political organization. To conquer his own kingdom while protecting it against Spanish incursions was no easy task; Henry's successes in 1598 constituted perhaps his greatest accomplishment. The Edict of Nantes (13 April) temporarily concluded civil warfare while the Peace of Vervins (2 May) brought the struggle against Spain to a close. But what did the Edict of Nantes mean for Protestants and Catholics?

---

[19] Cited in Steven Ozment, *The Age of Reform, 1250-1550: An Intellectual and Religious History of Late Medieval and Reformation Europe* (New Haven and London, 1980), 371.

[20] Michel de Montaigne, *The Complete Essays of Montaigne,* trans. Donald M. Frame (Stanford, 1965), 790.

[21] Monter, *Ritual, Myth and Magic,* 130; Lecler, *Toleration and the Reformation,* 2:479; Kamen, *The Rise of Toleration,* 121-22, 143-44.

In "The Crown, the Huguenots, and the Edict of Nantes," N. M. Sutherland takes a very close look at that Edict and then traces the relations between the monarchy and the Huguenots to 1629. Sutherland's topic is not new, but she dispels many of the myths surrounding it.[22]

Myth number one: the Edict was "a good thing" that worked during the reign of that good king, Henry IV. In fact, the Edict never worked; neither the Huguenots nor the Catholics accepted it as permanent. The lower clergy and the *parlements* in particular vilified the Edict;[23] the Catholic population considered the Protestants religiously indigestible. Exhaustion from eight civil wars spanning four decades led the crown, Huguenots, and Catholics to agree to the temporary expedient that was the Edict of Nantes. There had been similar edicts during the earlier wars between the Catholics and Protestants.[24] Why would any sixteenth-century Frenchman believe that the first "revocations"[25] of previous decades were exceptional? Moreover, Sutherland in her careful analysis proves that the Edict could not possibly have worked. It intended to destroy the Huguenot political organization (see article 82), the very prop that might have supported a workable edict. Lastly, all disagreed on what exactly the Edict meant—with good reason, for, as Sutherland says, it "was nurtured in ambiguity and founded in obfuscation." The Edict was "wobbly and imperfect," an apple of discord thrown before Catholics and Huguenots.[26]

Myth number two: Henry was a good king who favored the Huguenots. After all, Henry had twice been a Protestant, before his abjurations in 1572 and 1593, and he owed much to the Huguenots. Only after his assassination in 1610 did the idea

---

[22] It would be ridiculous if not absurd to argue that all historians accept all of the myths I list, but many accept most of them. From my own experiences, I have learned that members of the general public interested in this subject have been exposed to the myths.

[23] Frederic J. Baumgartner, "The Catholic Opposition to the Edict of Nantes, 1598-1599," *Bibliothèque d'Humanisme et Renaissance*, 40 (1978): 528. Henry IV, a masterful politician, still managed to convince the *parlements* to accept the Edict, although that of Rouen did not register it until 1609.

[24] On the early edicts, see N. M. Sutherland, *The Huguenot Struggle for Recognition* (New Haven and London, 1980).

[25] Emmanuel Le Roy Ladurie, introduction to Bernard Cottret, *Terre d'exil. L'Angleterre et ses réfugiés français et wallons, de la Réforme à la Révocation de l'Édit de Nantes* (Paris, 1985), 8.

[26] Janine Garrisson, "Bancal, imparfait, exceptionnel: l'Édit de Nantes," *Réforme*, number 2084 (23 March 1985): 14.

of Henry as a hero emerge.[27] The legend continues. A recent historian remarked: "Only a monarch of his courage, wisdom and cunning could have issued the decree [the Edict of Nantes]—and enforced it."[28] But Henry's weakness, not his strength, led him to agree to the Edict and explains, as Sutherland says, why he failed to enforce the Edict in many respects. Ascending the throne in 1589, Henry realized after a further nine years of struggle that he was not sufficiently secure in his power to force his will upon either Protestants or extreme Catholics.

Far from favoring Protestantism, the Edict of Nantes represented a clear victory for Catholicism.[29] The edict re-established the Roman Catholic Church everywhere, even in those regions where the population was entirely Protestant. Everyone, even Huguenots, had to pay the tithe to the Roman Church. Property confiscated from the Catholic Church was to be returned and priests and monks went back to areas from which Huguenots had expelled them. The Edict forbade Huguenots to preach or practice their religion outside certain areas, while the Catholic Church could expand throughout France. This cleared the path for the Counter Reformation, or Catholic Renaissance, in the first half of the seventeenth century; instead of fighting with arms, Catholics fought with tongues and pens. Missionary activity, reformed monasteries, new religious orders, the establishment of seminaries for priests—in these and other ways a revitalized Catholicism now opposed a wary and defensive Protestantism.[30]

Myth number three: the aim of the Edict was religious toleration. Sutherland states forcefully: "Peace was the purpose of the Edict, not toleration, which was neither a virtue nor an ideal." The Edict, after all, was extracted from Henry IV during France's war with Spain; he acted because he wanted peace at home, and not because he believed in the virtues of toleration. On the other hand, the Huguenots did receive

---

[27] Roland Mousnier, *The Assassination of Henry IV* (London, 1973), 240ff.

[28] Noel B. Gerson, *The Edict of Nantes* (New York, 1969), 16.

[29] This point is sometimes, but not often made. Mousnier, *The Assassination of Henry IV*, 148-49; Labrousse, *"Une foi, une loi, un roi?"* 30.

[30] One measure of the intensity of the continuing struggle was the proliferation of pamphlets and books that each religious camp directed against the other. During the thirty years after the Edict of Nantes, there were at least 3595 such works, with another 3471 appearing between 1629 and the Revocation. Louis Desgraves, ed., *Répertoire des ouvrages de controverse entre Catholiques et Protestants en France (1598-1685)*, 2 vols. (Geneva, 1984), 1:i. The Huguenots were at a serious disadvantage because of the Edict of Nantes, their small numbers, and the crown's blessings heaped on the Catholic side.

a measure of religious freedom. The Edict granted them the right to worship in certain places; this system of religious apartheid[31] was a form of toleration, even though based on expediency. "A government practices toleration if it allows religious minorities who do not conform to the established religion to live within its territory."[32] Sutherland rightly denies that the intent of the Edict was toleration, yet toleration—in the sense of the legal coexistence of two religions—was reaffirmed. (Toleration in this sense had first appeared in France in the Edict of Saint-Germain, January 1562.) We who revere toleration—the acceptance of different views, of the right of others to be, in our opinion, wrong—can applaud the Edict as renewing toleration. But it was not even the most tolerant edict of the civil wars—the Edict of Beaulieu in 1576, for example, allowed the public worship of the Reformed Religion in all Protestant areas and anywhere else by consent.[33] And, we cannot praise the intentions of the two religions granted legal existence, not of the Catholics, who vituperated the Edict of Nantes, and not of the Huguenots, who immediately violated its provisions.

Myth number four: the Edict of Nantes conferred political privileges. Here Sutherland is quite original, for some historians have been content to follow in the footsteps of Émile-G. Léonard, the great historian of French Protestantism, in asserting that the Edict made Protestantism politically privileged but religiously disfavored.[34] Tied to this is the common interpretation that the Edict created a Huguenot "state within a state." On the contrary, says Sutherland, the Edict did away with the Huguenot "state." She emphasizes the confusion between political privileges, which the Edict did not supply, and the many political consequences of the Edict. Thus the Edict forbade the Huguenots their political assemblies and the means to wage war. The holding of illegal assemblies after 1598 had serious political ramifications and

---

[31] This did not extend to social interaction; mixed marriages, family relationships, daily contacts, and opposition to the government ensured that some Catholics and Protestants would get along at the local level. Labrousse, *"Une foi, une loi, un roi?"* 81ff.

[32] Guggisberg, "The Defence of Religious Liberty in Early Modern Europe," 36. See also W. J. Stankiewicz, *Politics and Religion in Seventeenth-Century France* (Berkeley and Los Angeles, 1960), 1ff., 51, 63.

[33] Sutherland, *The Huguenot Struggle for Recognition*, 361.

[34] Émile-G. Léonard, "Le Protestantisme français au XVIIe siècle," *Revue historique*, 200 (October-December 1948): 155. As examples of some who have accepted this interpretation, see Menna Prestwich, "Calvinism in France, 1559-1629," in *International Calvinism, 1541-1715*, ed. Menna Prestwich (Oxford, 1985), 100; Daniel Ligou, "La peau de chagrin (1598-1685)," in Robert Mandrou et al., *Histoire des Protestants en France* (Toulouse, 1977), 118.

was a factor leading to the wars during the 1620s between the crown and the Huguenots.

Myth number five: Louis XIII (1610-43) ruined the Edict of Nantes, aided by his first minister, Cardinal Richelieu (1585-1642), who worked ardently to destroy the Huguenots. Although he took seriously his title of "Most Christian King" and presided over the flowering of the Catholic Renaissance, Louis XIII renewed repeatedly the Edict of Nantes. His infamous reputation, from the Huguenot point of view, emerged out of the wars of 1620-22, 1625-26, and 1627-29. The first was occasioned by Louis's entry in Béarn, a region in southwestern France not included in the Edict of Nantes. The conquest of Béarn, which had repudiated a royal edict of 1617, represented, according to Sutherland, "an act of authority, and not of persecution or of war." In 1621 and 1622 Louis exerted his authority once more by moving against the rebellious Huguenots in the south. The Peace of Montpellier made Louis master of about one-half of the 150 so-called hostage towns that the Edict of Nantes had granted the Huguenots,[35] but the peace guaranteed the religious provisions of the Edict, which Louis confirmed at least fifteen times. This pattern recurred in the armed struggle between the monarchy and the Huguenots that culminated in the seizure in 1628 of that great Protestant stronghold on the Atlantic, La Rochelle. Here again, Protestant rebellions resulted in royal victories. While lasting little more than a year, the Peace of La Rochelle that ended the rebellion of 1625-26 was rather moderate, almost favorable to the Huguenots. Devout Catholics rather than Huguenots had cause to be infuriated with such a treaty. The Edict or Grace of Alais (Alès) in 1629 concluded the war of 1627-29 and the Huguenots' control of hostage towns. This was a royal pardon: Louis did not punish individual Huguenots and, of course, he respected the religious and civil clauses of the Edict of Nantes.[36]

A man with strong religious convictions, working for the greater glory of the Catholic Church,[37] Richelieu nonetheless did not desire military campaigns in the south. Sutherland points out that he was too concerned with affairs of foreign policy,

---

[35] A royal *brevet* actually specified the hostage towns. Sutherland (*The Huguenot Struggle for Recognition*) describes the make-up (itself a source of confusion) of the Edict of Nantes.

[36] On these treaties, see also Victor-L. Tapié, *France in the Age of Louis XIII and Richelieu* (Cambridge, 1984), 152-53, 200-201.

[37] Cf. William F. Church, *Richelieu and Reason of State* (Princeton, 1972).

especially in northern Italy, to consider launching a crusade against the Huguenots. The Huguenots forced Richelieu's hand with their uprisings.

No, says Sutherland, the Huguenots could not blame Louis XIII or Richelieu for the collapse of their military structure at the close of the 1620s. They now stood defenseless before an increasingly absolutist state; that was the price for their three decades of violating the Edict of Nantes.

Sutherland's essay ends in 1629, when the Huguenots had lost their fortifications and their military protectors, the nobility, who had for the most part converted. What amazes, then, is not that the government revoked the Edict of Nantes, but that it revoked the Edict so late. Ever since the death of Henry IV, revocation was "in the air."[38] So was intolerance in the seventeenth century. France waited rather late to join the continent-wide trend. Spain expelled the Moriscos in 1611; Transylvania became a Protestant state; Catholicism gradually regained Poland; the Holy Roman Emperor crushed Protestantism in Bohemia during the 1620s; penal laws multiplied against English Catholics. Nevertheless, confessional pluralism continued in some places, such as the Holy Roman Empire and Switzerland. The United Provinces contained several religions. The imposition of religious uniformity slowed in England during the Puritan Revolution of the 1640s and 1650s as radical religious groups sprang up to demand their right to exist. The restoration of Charles II in 1660, however, ended the short period of relative toleration.[39]

In France, the Huguenots after 1629 remained in an impossible situation. There were two options. First, they could become more absolutist than the monarchy, calming kings with their obsequiousness. Second, they could attempt to make themselves feared, as Huguenots had done during the wars of religion. Neither of the two strategies would have prevented the nearly inevitable Revocation, but the simultaneous implementation of the two approaches proved to be a disaster.[40] Eventually, by the time of the mid-century revolts known as the *Frondes,* the majority of Huguenots

---

[38] Léonard, "Le Protestantisme français," 173.

[39] Monter, *Ritual, Myth and Magic,* 130-45; Kamen, *The Rise of Toleration,* 199-201; Le Roy Ladurie, introduction to Cottret, *Terre d'exil,* 9. The standard work on England is W. K. Jordan, *The Development of Religious Toleration in England,* 4 vols. (London, 1932-40).

[40] Labrousse, *"Une foi, une loi, un roi?"* 59.

opted for a position of ostentatious loyalty toward the crown, which thanked them in the Declaration of Saint-Germain in 1652 for their fidelity during the previous rebellions.

The Declaration provided a false sense of security; the Huguenots always fared better, in the sense that they were more likely to be left alone, during periods of warfare or revolt. France fought in the Thirty Years' War from 1635 to 1648, and war with Spain continued to 1659. The War of Devolution (1667-68) and the Dutch War (1672-78) occupied Louis's military during the first half of his reign. In addition, there were numerous military actions, notably the occupation of the Comtat Venaissin (1663) and of Lorraine (1664), the annexation of Strasbourg (1681), and an invasion of the Spanish Netherlands (1683). Two developments freed Louis's hands and contributed to the Huguenots' doom: the great period of peasant revolts, begun around 1625, ended by 1675; and the signing by France and the Holy Roman Emperor in 1684 of the Treaty of Ratisbon, which provided for a twenty years' truce.

Since the beginning of his personal reign in 1661, Louis XIV had as a goal the destruction of the *Religion prétendue réformée* (*R.P.R.*), the "self-styled reformed religion," as the French Catholics disparagingly labeled the French Calvinist (Reformed) religion. Louis applied restrictive, but not as yet persecuting measures against the Huguenots.[41] It must be emphasized that Louis was above all concerned with uniformity—political, cultural, and religious—and with his own *gloire,* his reputation.[42] These two concerns, along with his opportunism, go far toward explaining his revoking of the Edict of Nantes in 1685.

Bearing in mind that the situation varied from province to province, we can conveniently group Louis's policies toward the Huguenots into several distinct stages.[43] The period from 1661 to 1669 was one of hesitation and remission, with some use of force. Although the crown renewed the Edict of Nantes in 1662, the previous year had seen the first major use of the *dragonnades* (though only in a restricted area)

[41] Daniel Robert, "Louis XIV et les protestants," *XVIIe siècle*, 76-77 (1967): 40.

[42] The two best biographies of Louis XIV underscore his preoccupation with unity and *gloire.* John B. Wolf, *Louis XIV* (New York, 1968); Jean-Pierre Labatut, *Louis XIV. Roi de gloire* (Paris, 1984).

[43] Robert, "Louis XIV et les protestants," 41-44; Daniel Ligou, *Le Protestantisme en France de 1598 à 1715* (Paris, 1968), 208. Ligou's stages are more nuanced.

and the beginning of the demolition of those Protestant temples constructed since 1596-97. The government adopted the principle that whatever had not been specifically permitted in the Edict of Nantes was forbidden. (This narrow interpretation of the Edict of Nantes reminds one, ironically, of the Calvinist belief that whatever religious practice the Bible did not specifically allow was prohibited.) Also in the 1660s, Catholics who converted to Protestantism were punished, and there were attempts to raise Protestant children as Catholics. Other decrees prohibited the singing of Protestant psalms in the street (or even inside a temple, if a Catholic procession passed by), restricted Protestant funeral processions and burials, hindered Huguenots in the professions, and attempted to close Protestant schools.[44] A declaration in 1669 renewing important clauses of the Edict of Nantes marked a hiatus, though another government decree denied Huguenots the right to leave France without permission. The Revocation was also to refuse—except to pastors, who had two weeks—the *jus emigrandi*, the right to emigrate with one's personal property. This provision was to make the Revocation particularly heinous; the Peace of Westphalia, which had renewed the principle of *cuius regio, eius religio* and extended it to Calvinism, had granted religious minorities in Germany the *jus emigrandi*.[45]

Relative détente marked the second stage, lasting until 1678-79. Preoccupied with the Dutch War, the government allowed the Huguenots to twist slowly in the wind. The innovation during the period was the creation in 1676 of the *Caisse des Économats* (referred to by the Huguenots as the Bureau of Conversions), headed by a former Protestant, Paul Pellisson (1624-93). Pensions, appointments, and favors had bought off most of the Huguenot aristocracy earlier in the century; now the crown offered money to Huguenots lower on the social scale if they would convert.

The final stage distinguished itself by violence and culminated when Louis XIV—his hands free of foreign entanglements, himself undergoing a "conversion" experience—was able to concentrate on the Huguenot problem and rid himself of the stain on his reputation as a Catholic king. Now the monarchy interpreted the Edict of Nantes as stringently as possible, forbidding mixed marriages and prohibiting

---

[44] Labrousse, *"Une foi, une loi, un roi?"* 138ff.

[45] Ibid., 98, 196-99; Elisabeth Labrousse, "Calvinism in France, 1598-1685," in *International Calvinism, 1541-1715*, p. 305.

18

Huguenots from entering many trades. The government closed the last of the Protestant academies. The destruction of temples continued; from perhaps 600-700 in
1660, approximately one hundred remained in 1680. Catholics were no longer allowed to convert to Protestantism. On the other hand, Catholic midwives
(Protestants could not now become midwives) were permitted to baptize the Protestant newborn, while priests hurried to the deathbeds of Huguenots for a final effort
at conversion. The list of declarations against the Huguenots is too long to mention
here (no one has yet made an exhaustive study); let it suffice that on the eve of the
Revocation there were so many restrictive measures that a Huguenot would have
found it almost impossible not to be in violation of one law or another.[46]

The first of the great *dragonnades* took place in Poitou in 1681. Their use was
not new; they had been employed before against Huguenots and most recently in
1675 at the occasion of a peasant uprising in Brittany. But now their use became
general in an attempt to force conversions. In a few months, thirty to thirty-five
thousand Huguenots abjured in Poitou, three times more than Pellisson had garnered
in three years from the entire kingdom.[47] A few Catholics may have had reservations
about this vicious force, but the *dragonnades* did work. They continued, sporadically,
in several provinces, climaxing in June and July 1685. Of the 22,000 Huguenots in
Béarn, 21,500 converted. In Montauban alone, 17,600 converted in six days.[48] After
such successes, Louis XIV could well believe that he could revoke the Edict of Nantes
without serious consequences; with hardly any Huguenots remaining, there was no
need for the Edict.

In her essay, "Understanding the Revocation of the Edict of Nantes from the
Perspective of the French Court," Elisabeth Labrousse examines the crown's motives
and attitudes. Louis XIV's central role has been the subject of many works. The
eminent French historian, Jean Orcibal, has argued that foreign affairs, more than

---

[46] Of the laws passed against the Huguenots, see Labrousse, *"Une foi, une loi, un roi?"* 167ff; Janine
Garrisson, *L'Édit de Nantes et sa révocation. Histoire d'une intolérance* (Paris, 1985), 127ff. A good,
short summary is in E. Préclin and E. Jarry, *Les Luttes politiques et doctrinales aux XVIIe et XVIIIe
siècles* (Paris, 1955), 125-26.

[47] Jean Quéniart, *La Révocation de l'Édit de Nantes. Protestants et catholiques français de 1598 à 1685*
(Paris, 1985), 118-19.

[48] L. L. Bernard, "Foucault, Louvois, and the Revocation of the Edict of Nantes," *Church History*, 25
(March 1956): 35; Préclin and Jarry, *Les Luttes politiques et doctrinales*, 127.

any other factor, explain the decision to revoke the Edict of Nantes in October 1685.[49] Certainly, the Truce of Ratisbon (1684) with the emperor removed the immediate prospect of war. Protestant princes in Germany no longer perceived the emperor as a threat to their independence, so France was free to dismantle her system of alliances with Protestant states. This was a dramatic break in French foreign policy, for those states and Catholic France had been, off and on, uneasy bedfellows since the reign of Francis I (1515-47). In 1685, the Catholic James II (1685-88) ascended the throne of England; Louis now posed as his protector. Moreover, the French had not joined with other Europeans at the Battle of Kahlenberg (1683), when the Ottoman Turks were defeated outside Vienna. Louis's *gloire* was tarnished; he needed something brilliant, something grandiose that would redeem his reputation as the Most Christian King. What could be more opportune than an end to the Huguenot problem? This would have the added advantage of forcing Pope Innocent XI (1676-89) to congratulate the French king. Louis had quarreled with various popes since the beginning of his personal reign; most recently, he and the pope had been at loggerheads over the question of the *régale* (the right to the revenues of certain vacant benefices) and over the monarch's extreme Gallicanism (the right of the French Church to maintain a degree of independence from Rome).

Labrousse recognizes the significance of foreign affairs, but her emphasis lies elsewhere than on Louis's opportunism. She makes the point that, whereas the object of the Revocation was religious (the destruction of the *R.P.R.*), the objective was political (security in the state through the elimination of a danger to the monarchy). This interpretation gives symmetry to the view that foreign policy considerations were uppermost in Louis's mind. Implicit in Labrousse's interpretation is that Louis acted for political motives related both to internal and external affairs. Internally, Louis and the court feared the Huguenot political cancer that ate at the French state. Aquinas's viral theory, offered as a rationale to cut out religious heresy, was now applied to political heresy. The Huguenots, Labrousse argues, were infected with the republican disease. The court did not distinguish between French Huguenots and English Protestant regicides who had mercilessly executed King Charles I (1625-49) and established a commonwealth. How could an absolutist ruler look with

[49] Jean Orcibal, *Louis XIV et les Protestants* (Paris, 1951); Orcibal, "Louis XIV and the Edict of Nantes," in *Louis XIV and Absolutism*, ed. Ragnhild Hatton (Columbus, Ohio, 1976), 154-76.

equanimity upon a group of subjects, who, despite their repeated protestations of loyalty, seemed clearly to harbor republican ideas? The internal church organization of the *R.P.R.* offered proof of democracy in action, of a whiff of egalitarianism anathema to a king perched on top of the social pyramid and committed to preserving the structure of a hierarchy in which subjects belonged to groups and corporations that were decidedly unequal. If the Huguenots denied they had democratic tendencies and proclaimed their fidelity to the monarchy, the court knew the truth lay elsewhere. Huguenots in the sixteenth century had revolted against the monarchy and defended the right to resist; there was no good reason to believe Huguenots in the 1680s were any different. The crown still saw its Protestant subjects as rebels and trouble-makers. The country had to be made safe for absolutism.

According to this perspective, then, the Revocation was an act of political rather than of religious intolerance. In fact, the Edict of Fontainebleau did not revoke any notion of tolerance because none had existed in the first place in France. The Edict of Nantes had provided for the coexistence, the toleration of two legal religions, but never was intended to be an expression of tolerance. Labrousse strengthens her case by showing that the Huguenots came to be described as schismatics, rather than as heretics. In keeping with the mental gymnastics practiced at the time, the court and clergy were thus able to argue—having the authority of Saint Augustine on their side—that the crown could legitimately compel the Huguenots to return to the Catholic religion. The Revocation became the climactic political event of the French Counter Reformation.

As Labrousse demonstrates, there were other advantages to the Revocation from the court's perspective. The government had enticed the "New Converts" (Huguenots who had recently become Catholic) with tax exemptions. Not only did the monarchy suffer subsequently from a decrease in tax revenue, but the weight of taxation fell increasingly upon longstanding Catholics. The Revocation neatly solved this difficulty. Also, the Revocation served the purpose of doing away with the morass of laws enacted against the Huguenots, cumbersome and often inapplicable laws that themselves became part of the problem rather than a solution.

Labrousse's essay raises the question of the amount of blame that should be assigned to the two favorite objects of historians' scorn, Louis XIV and the Catholic clergy. She states that the king, from the court's vantage point, was no despot. He had every right to proceed against his Huguenot subjects. Another factor, not discussed by Labrousse, is relevant here. Louis experienced a religious crisis at mid-reign. Notwithstanding a marriage in the first year of his personal rule, unquestioning acceptance of Catholic dogma, and a conscientious religious formalism, Louis had been somewhat of a rake (to the chagrin of his wife, mother, and court preachers). In the 1680s, Louis underwent a religious conversion (though that might be too strong a term). His last mistress died in 1680; he then returned to his wife, Maria Theresa, took frequent communion, and even prohibited opera and comedy during Lent. After Maria Theresa died in 1683, the king married Madame de Maintenon and apparently remained faithful to her. Louis became devout and the court quickly followed suit.[50] What better way to assuage his conscience for the personal disorders that had characterized his life than to eliminate that great disorder and patent offense to god, the *R.P.R.*? Contemporaries recognized the connection between the Revocation and Louis's discovery of personal morality. One wrote that Louis believed that the persecution of the Huguenots assured him of "merit, capable of atoning for his past disorders, in the eyes of God and the Roman Church."[51]

Guilty of deceiving Louis in their depiction of the Huguenots, the Catholic clergy nonetheless behaved as their position seemed to require. Products of the seminaries created according to the decrees of the Council of Trent, these ecclesiastics were true to the religious ethos of the seventeenth-century French Catholic Renaissance. They could be expected to remain unsatisfied until the *R.P.R.* had become extinct. Indeed, throughout the century, the general assembly of the clergy (the quinquennial meeting of representatives of the French Catholic Church), hovering in the background like a Greek chorus, repeatedly begged the king to act against the Protestants.[52] Labrousse does find the clergy, because of their bitter hatred for the Huguenots, suffering from a "moral fault," but her interpretation of the clergy is balanced—she seeks to understand, not simply to judge.

[50] Ligou, *Le Protestantisme en France de 1598 à 1715*, pp. 211-12.

[51] Cited in Labatut, *Louis XIV*, 270.

[52] Pierre Blet, *Le Clergé de France et la monarchie. Étude sur les Assemblées du Clergé de 1615 à 1666*, 2 vols. (Rome, 1959), 2:342-88, 404-405; Blet, *Les Assemblées du Clergé et Louis XIV de 1670 à 1693* (Rome, 1972), 423ff.

Labrousse claims that royal policies failed because the monarchy was not strong enough to impose its will. This is ironic, as government weakness had led to the Edict of Nantes in the first place. The absolutist state developed over the course of the seventeenth century; by 1685 it was much more powerful than it had been in 1598. The problem lay in that the monarchy was sufficiently absolute to issue the Revocation, but not so to excoriate the Huguenots. Both sides suffered from delusion: Huguenots thought their fawning before Louis XIV and acceptance of divine-right monarchy would save them from the Revocation, while the crown believed it could easily bring the Huguenots back into the Catholic fold.

The Edict of Fontainebleau itself is quite short, consisting of a preamble and twelve articles (see Appendix II). In the preamble, Louis XIV stated that Henry's premature death had prevented him from carrying out his intention to reunite the Church, while Louis XIII had been hindered by foreign wars. Now Louis, finally free from international warfare owing to the Truce of Ratisbon in 1684, was in a position to revoke the Edict of Nantes.[53] Article I specifically revoked the Edict of Nantes and decreed that all remaining Protestant temples be demolished. The present Edict, like the one it superseded, was declared "perpetual and irrevocable." The second and third articles prohibited Protestant worship and forbade Protestant noblemen to hold religious services in their homes or fiefs. Article IV ordered the expulsion of Protestant pastors from France within fifteen days, while article V offered financial rewards to those pastors who would convert. Article VI made it easier for former pastors to become lawyers. The seventh article closed schools for Protestant children and the eighth article ordered those children baptized and raised as Catholics. Article IX permitted Huguenots who had already fled France to return within four months to regain their property, which otherwise would be confiscated. Article X forbade Huguenots to leave the kingdom or send out their property, under penalty of the galleys for men and imprisonment for women. Article XI retained the prior laws against relapsed Catholics. The final article is difficult to understand, for it permitted Huguenots liberty of conscience if they did not practice their religion.[54] The Revocation did not force the Huguenots to abjure; Louis was prepared to wait for god to

---

[53] The Revocation did not apply to Alsace, still regulated by the Peace of Augsburg (1555).

[54] "On s'est perdu en conjectures sur le sens de ce texte." Ligou, *Le Protestantisme en France de 1598 à 1715*, p. 248.

enlighten the remaining ones. Perhaps the court believed that, left without an organized church, Huguenots would be unable to continue in their religion or that, perhaps, the final article would mollify the anger of Protestant states.[55] In any case, article XII did not atone for the rigor of the other articles, and it certainly did not impede the quartering of dragoons in Huguenot households after the Revocation.

Huguenots had fled France in the sixteenth century, but the Revocation and the coercive acts leading up to it impelled one-fifth of French Protestants, about 1 percent of the population of France, to emigrate. These refugees had great courage (and usually geographical proximity to France's frontiers), for they had to risk their lives, forsake property, family, friends, and their homeland, and suffer a perilous journey that, if it did not result in capture and terrible punishment, could easily end in a marginal, penniless existence in an alien culture.

The Huguenots fled mainly to neighboring Protestant territories: as many as 70,000 to the United Provinces, 30-40,000 to Germany, 40-50,000 to Great Britain, and 20,000 to Switzerland. Another 2,000 settled in Denmark and other parts of northern Europe, while 1,500-2,000 eventually went to the American Colonies.[56] In the New World, South Carolina became known as the "home of the Huguenots."[57]

Jon Butler's essay, "The Revocation of the Edict of Nantes and Huguenot Migration to South Carolina," stresses the close connection between the Revocation itself and the lives of those French Protestants who braved the Atlantic crossing to live in the colony of South Carolina. Women figured prominently among the refugees leaving France and, later, among those who came to South Carolina. Because the Revocation forbade Huguenots from throughout France to leave, refugee communities were quite cosmopolitan in comparison with the Protestant congregations existing

---

[55] Orcibal, *Louis XIV et les Protestants*, 112; Labrousse, *"Une foi, une loi, un roi?"* 199.

[56] I have looked at figures from Philippe Joutard, "The Revocation of the Edict of Nantes: End or Renewal of French Calvinism?" in *International Calvinism, 1541-1715*, pp. 352-55; Gwynn, *Huguenot Heritage*, 24, 35; G. C. Gibbs, "Some Intellectual and Political Influences of the Huguenot Emigrés in the United Provinces, c. 1680-1730," *Bijragenen en Mededlingen betreffende de Geschiedenis der Nederlanden*, 90 (1975): 256, Hans Bot and René Bastiaanse, "Le Refuge Huguenot et les Provinces-Unies, une esquisse sommaire," in *Le Refuge Huguenot*, eds. Michelle Magdelaine and Rudolf von Thadden (Paris, 1985), 64: Jon Butler, *The Huguenots in America: A Refugee People in New World Society* (Cambridge, Mass., 1983), 49.

[57] Charles Weiss, *History of the French Protestant Refugees, from the Revocation of the Edict of Nantes to Our Own Days*, 2 vols. (New York, 1854), 2:336.

in France before 1685. Moreover, because the brutal treatment of French Protestants both preceded and followed the Revocation, Huguenots left France in droves throughout the 1680s. (Indeed, the ship *Richmond*, sailing from England in 1679, brought the first official colony of Huguenots to South Carolina in 1680.)[58] This decade-long emigration, Butler argues, meant that the refugee communities were in constant flux, lacking stability.

Deprived of their property in France, Huguenot emigrants often had experienced dire poverty before arriving in South Carolina; it was that poverty that induced many refugees to choose South Carolina. Promotional literature provided a glowing description of the economic opportunities South Carolina had to offer. Butler cites a letter from Louis Thibou, dated 20 September 1683, that describes a temperate climate, plentiful and good food, and a colony where a man with half the income could live as well as a gentleman in France (see Appendix III). Here is the first of the ironies that make the Huguenot refugees in South Carolina so fascinating: having left France for purely religious considerations, they chose South Carolina for economic reasons. The Huguenot diaspora may well have been the first wave of emigration for ideological reasons,[59] but this secondary migration—from England, usually, to South Carolina—reflected little of the religious zeal of those who had trooped from France in the wake of Louis's dragoons.

How quickly South Carolina Huguenots threw off their religious heritage! As Butler describes, pro-Anglican sympathies appeared among the clergymen, then among other Huguenots.[60] Although there was a brief resistance, Anglican conformity consumed much of the Huguenot population. In the eighteenth century, the religious assimilation of the Huguenots was nearly complete, as many moved beyond Anglicanism to join other Protestant denominations.

Socially and economically, South Carolina Huguenots also distanced themselves from their French past. Least innocuously, Huguenots abandoned their traditional

---

[58] Martha Bailey Burns, "The Richmond," The Huguenot Society of South Carolina, *Transactions*, 85 (1980): 43-49.

[59] Joutard, "The Revocation of the Edict of Nantes," 345.

[60] Cf. Robert M. Kingdon, "Why Did the Huguenot Refugees in the American Colonies Become Episcopalian?" *Historical Magazine of the Protestant Episcopal Church*, 49 (December 1980): 317-35.

trades by the turn of the eighteenth century. Perhaps anxious to forget their poverty and need for charity in England, South Carolina Huguenots quickly acquired land, on a scale much greater than that of any other immigrant group in the American colonies. Overall, the Huguenots met enormous success, overcoming their initial disadvantages and the sometime discrimination they encountered from the English colonists. The publicity extolling South Carolina as a land of milk and honey proved to be correct.

Most indicative of the Huguenots' economic success and Americanization was their slaveholding. This is Butler's major point and the great anomaly between what the Huguenots were in seventeenth-century France and what they became in eighteenth-century South Carolina. Nearly all Huguenot men purchased slaves, often in great numbers. Slaveholding became, among the Huguenots, almost the *sine qua non* for Americanization. Like the early Christians and sixteenth-century Protestants, the eighteenth-century Huguenots in South Carolina failed a power test. Stripped of their freedom to worship and persecuted by Louis XIV, the Huguenots had no qualms whatsoever in owning slaves. Conscious of their own sufferings—there is a large body of literature by Huguenots about the French government's atrocities, such as the *dragonnades* or the galleys—Huguenots were remarkably insensitive to the sufferings of others. Butler is concerned to note that the Huguenots could have looked to criticisms of slavery by their coreligionists, but that surely did not suit their secular goals. Maybe those criticisms—by the Rouen synod in 1637, for instance—constituted the greatest anomaly. After all, the Huguenots came from a hierarchical society, one steeped in an ethos of inequality. Perhaps Butler is too severe on those Huguenots who emigrated to South Carolina; one might also contend that the demand for religious toleration is quite unrelated to whether or not one possesses human chattels. Be that as it may, the Huguenots began their purchase of slaves while Calvinists, but their becoming Anglicans, Methodists, or Baptists did not alter their behavior. All these religions in Colonial America had affinity, not with the pronouncement of the Rouen synod, but with Martin Luther, who condemned the German peasant revolt of 1524-25 with these rancorous words:

> There should be no serfs, because Christ has freed us all! What is this we hear? That is to make Christian freedom wholly bodily. Did not Abraham and the other patriarchs and prophets have serfs? Read what St. Paul says of servants, who in all times have been serfs. So this article is straight against the gospel. . . . This article would make all

men equal and convert the spiritual kingdom of Christ into an external wordly one; but that is impossible, for a worldly realm cannot stand where there is no inequality; some must be free, others bond. . . .[61]

Thoroughly Christianized (in the sense that the truth of Christianity is the history of Christianity),[62] the Huguenots simply became Americanized.

We return, then, to the question of why the Revocation should be commemorated. Because, affirms Butler, it affected everything it touched. The Revocation was unusually significant. The three essays in this book may cause chagrin for those who prefer to see the Huguenots as blameless defenders of liberty, a minority fighting to preserve religious freedom against bigoted Catholicism and Machiavellian absolutism. Beyond the examples of individual heroics, there is precious little that is admirable in this story. Sutherland does not even allow us to commemorate the Revocation in order to celebrate the Edict of Nantes, for she proves that the Huguenots extorted it and immediately flouted it. No group saw the Edict as definitive, as anything more than a temporary lull in the ceaseless battle between truth and error. As Sutherland argues, the Edict was unsatisfactory, unoriginal, uncreative, and not a positive act. Far from the persecution of the Huguenots being religious, it was, according to Labrousse, in large part political. The French court of Louis XIV saw the Huguenots as trouble-makers and rebels. As for blaming bigoted Catholicism, the Catholic clergy did the job expected of them; furthermore, one could not argue cogently that Huguenots were any less intolerant. The problem lay not in one side or the other, but in both Protestants and Catholics. Historically, dogmatism and intolerance have been basic features of Christianity.[63]

The three essays in this book say nothing to dispute this. The intolerance can not even be ascribed to monarchy and political absolutism; there was no necessary link between political absolutism and religious intolerance. James II, the "one truly absolutist Stuart king,"[64] was also the most religiously tolerant of England's seven-

---

[61] Cited in James H. Robinson, *Readings in European History*, 2 vols. (Boston, 1906), 2:99-100.

[62] Jeffery Burton Russell, *The Devil: Perceptions of Evil from Antiquity to Primitive Christianity* (Ithaca and London, 1977), 221.

[63] Michael Mullett, *Radical Religious Movements in Early Modern Europe* (London, 1980), 76.

[64] Kamen, *The Rise of Toleration*, 216.

teenth-century rulers.[65] Indeed, the history of toleration shows that toleration usually filtered from the top of society to the masses, who were often the most enthusiastic proponents of religious and social conformity. It would take the slow diffusion, beginning in the eighteenth century, of a new secular and humanitarian ethic, one centered on empathy, for the hydra of religious intolerance to lose its last, ugly head.

---

[65] Of course, James, a Catholic king in a Protestant country, found it in his interests to recognize dissenting Protestants. His Protestant subjects opposed this toleration because it would benefit Roman Catholics. See Elisabeth Labrousse, "1685 et 1688," in *La Tolérance. XIIIe Colloque de l'Institut de Recherche sur la civilisation de l'Occident Moderne* (Paris, 1985), 25-31.

THE CROWN, THE HUGUENOTS, AND THE EDICT OF NANTES

N. M. Sutherland

In 1985, we observed the tercentenary of the Revocation of the Edict of Nantes.[1] The Edict represents the recognition, according to specified conditions, of a Calvinist minority within the state and society of France. But it should be realized that the Edict revoked in 1685 was no longer that of 1598, which had undergone a protracted process of emasculation. Its withdrawal was not a sudden act of juridical violence, though it might be considered a counterproductive error. This is already to pose a number of problems and questions about the Huguenots and the nature of the Edict, its permanency, and the extent to which that minority had thereby been accepted. Acceptance cannot be ensured by legislation, and permanency proves to be a slippery conception: something lasting, or intended to last indefinitely; durable but not eternal; nothing lasts for ever. There were always conflicting opinions as to how long it could, would or should last.[2] The Huguenots' own restless efforts to obtain additional concessions did not suggest finality. For them their Edict was still a mere beginning. This all points to the existence of problems, and to instability and change. Furthermore, like everything else the Huguenots themselves had changed. Those who suffered the Revocation were quite unlike the bellicose aristocratic faction of the 1590s.[3]

The Revocation has generally had a bad press, perhaps because the ideology behind it has been less apparent than the high hostility divorced from any danger. Conversely, there seems to have been a traditional and simplistic assumption that the Edict was a good thing from a good king; that it worked under Henry IV and that the

---

[1] The Edict of Fontainebleau, 17 October 1685, really extended to all France conditions which already obtained in many parts. Charles Drion, *Histoire chronologique de l'église Protestante de France jusqu'à la révocation de l'édit de Nantes*, 2 vols. (Paris, 1855), 2:268-72.

[2] The Edict of Nantes was qualified as "irrevocable," which meant that it could only be revoked by another registered edict. Both parties are said to have seen it from the start as transitory and unstable. Émile-G. Léonard, "Le Protestantisme français au XVIIe siècle," *Revue historique*, 200 (October-December 1948): 155; Joseph Faurey, *L'Édit de Nantes et la question de tolérance* (Paris, 1929), 51.

[3] The changing social composition of the Huguenots is a major subject. The main lines of these changes have been indicated by Léonard, "Le Protestantisme français," 164-65.

Huguenots were ruined by Louis XIII before the Edict was revoked by his successor, Louis XIV.[4] Alongside these misconceptions lies a strong tendency to idolize Henry IV as the Protestants' savior, assuming his good relations with Huguenot devotees. On the contrary, their relations, which were already strained before his accession in 1589, turned hostile after his abjuration in 1593.[5] There is no doubt that the sufferings of a tenacious minority have been romanticized, although they were rather more prone to demand a tooth for a tooth than to turn the other cheek.[6] The Edict of Nantes never was that "good thing," the definitive settlement of a persistent problem, but rather an ultimate recognition of deadlock. Much error has arisen from thinking of the Edict in static terms, as something done, something there, and something wantonly destroyed. To be executed at all, the Edict had to be constantly interpreted. Thus even in juridical terms, it was never a precise instrument and we are really dealing with fluid, changing factors and conflicts, many or most of which were not religious. It was the polarization that was religious, as well as the powerful emotive content. Thus, if one looks more closely at the nature of the Edict and its turbulent progression from 1598 to 1629, when it was redefined, one is bound to suspect that the position of the crown and the Huguenots alike was basically untenable. Indeed, in vital respects the Edict was never to be observed, because it did not properly reflect the needs of either the crown or the Huguenots. It embodied a maximum of extortion on the one hand, and of concessions on the other, besides restoring the essentials of former edicts of pacification, in particular the Edict of Poitiers, 1577. That the Edict of Nantes was unoriginal has, predominantly, been ignored.[7]

---

[4] A. Poirson, for example, in his monumental history of Henry's reign, asserts that the Edict was not abused under Henry IV; this is patently false. He does not, however, say that the Edict was a good thing but rather that it was more derogatory to the power of the crown than the treaties with the Catholic League. *Histoire du règne de Henri IV*, 4 vols. (Paris, 1862-67), 2:521; F.-T. Perrens also asserts that the Edict brought Henry the support of the Huguenots. *L'Église et l'état en France sous le règne de Henri IV et la régence de Marie de Médicis*, 2 vols. (Paris, 1873), 1:143.

[5] This assumption of good relations may have derived in part from the fact that Huguenot theory came to support the crown, while resistance theories were adopted by the Catholics. Nevertheless, the Huguenots did resist. Harmut Kretzer, "Remarques sur le droit de résistance des Calvinistes français au début du XVIIè siècle," *Bulletin de la Société de l'Histoire du Protestantisme Français* (hereafter *BSHPF*), 123 (1977): 59-60.

[6] Schybergson, "Le duc de Rohan et le parti Protestant 1610-1622," *BHSPF*, 29 (1880): 52. He also mentions their venomous propaganda (ibid., 53).

[7] P. Beuzart, "L'Édit de Nantes, création ou aboutissement," *BHSPF*, 91 (1942), has compared the Edict of Nantes with the edicts of pacification. Janine Garrisson, *L'Édit de Nantes et sa révocation. Histoire d'une intolérance* (Paris, 1985), 17, has most recently made this point. See also, N. M. Sutherland, *The Huguenot Struggle for Recognition* (New Haven and London, 1980), 334-72, where all the edicts are analyzed.

If we are to ask why, then, did the Edict last "indefinitely," or for eighty-seven years, to be precise, the answers would be largely circumstantial. In particular, the juridical survival of the Huguenots became closely involved with faction struggles for power at court, foreign alliances and the defense of France; things which relate to the exploitation of political forces and not to matters of religion. There was no time before the beginning of the personal rule of Louis XIV in 1661 (he came to the throne in 1643 aged four) when it was politically possible to revoke the Edict. By then Europe was beyond the era of so-called "religious wars," and France past her era of the nobility in arms and opposition, with the intervention of Spain in her domestic affairs. Ensuing methods of coercion and conversion were therefore slower and more insidious. Nevertheless, to the most powerful forces in the kingdom, the Catholic Church and the sovereign courts (the *parlements*, which inherited the medieval inquisitorial function), the extinction of heresy, that blemish on the face of France, remained their ultimate objective.[8]

That the Edict should eventually be revoked was, in the nature of things, always a strong probability, if not ineluctable. But since, after 1629, the Huguenots were no longer linked with seditious forces, the matter was no longer urgent. By inheritance and policy, the king himself was committed to the Edict, although his mutable attitude was never more than tepidly correct. As late as 1652, Louis had ostensibly rewarded the Protestants' quiescence during the *Fronde*—the name given to grave disturbances of his minority—with a full reinstatement of the Edict of Nantes, as redefined in 1629, and the removal of subsequent executive restrictions.[9] This, however, is more likely to have reflected the government's need for support, money and alliances in time of war than the attitude of the king to his heretic subjects.[10] No longer

---

[8] Léonard, "Le Protestantisme français," 166, 170, 173, 174. The abiding position of the clergy was made clear at the estates general of 1614-15. They did not categorically demand the revocation of the Edict until 1665. Pierre Blet, *Le Clergé de France et la monarchie. Étude sur les Assemblées du Clergé de 1615 à 1666*, 2 vols. (Rome, 1959), 1:99ff., 2:342ff., 378ff.

[9] The Edict was twice renewed under Louis XIV: 8 July 1643 and 21 May 1652, which restored the Edict and all subsequent regulations in the Huguenots' favor registered by the *parlements*. Blet, *Le Clergé de France*, 2:346, 350; Léonard, "Le Protestantisme français," 169. The Declaration of 21 May 1652 was revoked on 11 January 1657. A *règlement* of 2 April 1666 codified in fifty-nine articles all the changes to the Edict since 1643 and was amplified on 1 February 1669. On 21 January 1669 and 4 July 1679 the (judicial) *chambres de l'édit* were suppressed. The Edict was eroded by a very large number of regulations relating, in particular, to the prohibition of the cult and the demolition of churches (temples); also to the exclusion of Protestants from offices, professions and occupations, and to the harassment of pastors. Drion, *Histoire chronologique*, 2:8-272 passim.

[10] Elisabeth Labrousse, *"Une foi, une loi, un roi?" La Révocation de l'Édit de Nantes* (Paris and Geneva, 1985), 41-42, relates the Declaration of 21 May 1652 to Mazarin's need for an English alliance.

a military faction, the Calvinists had penetrated the world of the financiers, upon whom the government depended.[11] Louis XIII, after much provocation, had finally observed a diminished Edict with legalistic severity, but the crown had not positively persecuted obedient heretics, at least in a juridical sense, since the death of Henry II in 1559.[12] Neither had it ever sufficiently protected them, whether before or after the Edict of Nantes. It really was not possible for any king of France to do so. These observations are again suggestive of problems, some inherent in the Edict itself, and some in the relations between the crown and the Huguenots which, in effect, the Edict did little or nothing to alter.

We have tended to think with relief of the Edict of Nantes and the Peace of Vervins with Spain, 1598, as ending the tangled wars of the sixteenth century. The treaties, however, were no more than symptomatic of the triumphs of the king, and just *how* victorious was the king? The treaty with Spain was really a truce, and if Henry did prevail in France, his supremacy was fragile and very ill-assured. Neither loyal to their old "Protector," nor yet his open enemies, the Huguenots are not to be seen as royal allies entering upon their birthright; neither were they a vanquished faction humbly receiving Henry's grace.

Peace was the purpose of the Edict, not toleration, which was neither a virtue nor an ideal. Furthermore, it was mainly the king who wanted peace, a *sine qua non* for the kingdom of France.[13] The Huguenots sought advantages, and among their divided ranks—for they were not an homogeneous group—there were always those who sought to profit from the renewal of war. To them the Edict of Nantes was not climacteric, but simply one more edict of pacification, none of which had been truly

---

[11] Léonard, "Le Protestantisme français," 168-69, points out that, excluded from offices in spite of their eligibility, the Huguenots made themselves indispensable in the financial milieu, and could not safely be alienated.

[12] One should perhaps distinguish between persecution, juridically speaking, and ill-treatment through a negative interpretation of the Edict. Roland Mousnier, *L'Assassinat d'Henri IV* (Paris, 1964), 133, said that, strictly applied, the Edict would become "un instrument de combat et d'étouffement." English translation by Joan Spencer (London, 1973).

[13] The king had reason to fear a further Huguenot rebellion, which underlines the point that the Huguenots were not a defeated faction. The Venetian ambassador stressed the king's need to conciliate them. Bergey de Xivrey, *Recueil des lettres missives de Henri IV*, 9 vols. (Paris, 1844-76), 4:825-26, 11 August 1597, Henry to the duc de Piney-Luxembourg, ambassador in Rome; 896, 11 January 1598, Henry to La Chastre; 947, 2 April 1598, Henry to the constable; *Calendar of State Papers Venetian, 1592-1603*, p. 301, 9 December 1597, Contarini to the doge.

accepted.[14] To his Catholic opponents, the king's rationale was necessity; this evoked an irritable resignation, still without true acceptance where a deep antipathy prevailed.[15] This interim attitude to the Edict was uneasily suggestive of termination, should the necessity ever cease.[16] So the Huguenots remained alert and were never fully pacified. Indeed Henry himself declared that it was only he who held the antagonists apart; and in that case everything depended on his life. This was also to imply that the principal conflict lay between the opposing factions, not between the Huguenots and the crown. On the other hand, the essential Huguenot/Catholic quarrel also fueled distrust of the crown in the form of a basic anxiety that a Catholic king was unreliable. Either way the Huguenots' only security lay in self-defense. In reality, the problem was less the Catholicism of the king, than his incomplete executive power. The Huguenots therefore had distanced the king at least since his abjuration in 1593. That was followed by generous capitulations with the towns and leaders of the Catholic League, an extreme political faction whose ultramontane spirit and hatred of the Huguenots did not instantly expire.

The new Edict, first demanded in 1594 by a defiant assembly at Sainte-Foy, was extorted, under duress, over several years in time of war.[17] It was therefore a piecemeal assortment of bargains, partly derogatory to the power of the crown, which did not terminate but simply redefined the conflict. To call it a negative achievement might be a little too extreme.[18] In superseding previous edicts it removed the dangers

---

[14] The Edict of Nantes was so described. Sutherland, *The Huguenot Struggle for Recognition*, is based on the successive edicts. The texts, excluding the Edict of Nantes, have been printed by A. Stegmann, *Édits des guerres de religion* (Paris, 1979).

[15] For the pope's benefit Henry explained: "La partie de ceux de contraire religion est encore trop enracinée ... et trop forte puissante dedans et dehors [l'état] pour estre mise à non chaloir," quoted by Faurey, *L'Edit de Nantes*, 25, 27, 28.

[16] This argument—no further necessity—was indeed made in the preamble to the Edict of Fontainebleau, 17 October 1685.

[17] N. M. Sutherland, "The Edict of Nantes and the Protestant State," *Annali della Fonaazione italiana per la storia amministrativa*, 2 (1965): 199-235, shows how the Edict was extorted. Confusion on this point still colors judgements of the Edict itself. René Taveneaux recently declared that the difference between Nantes and previous edicts was that "le roi a désormais la possibilité de proclamer sa volonté et de la faire appliquer." *Le Catholicisme dans la France classique 1610-1715*, 2 vols. (Paris, 1980), 1:24-5. The form and content of the Edict alone negate the first proposition. Long ago the Jesuit historian Gabriel Daniel roundly declared that the manner in which the Edict was obtained was alone sufficient to justify its revocation. *Histoire de France*, 10 vols. (Paris, 1729), 10:212. To the Catholics the Edict was a truce. Jean Orcibal, *Louis XIV et les protestants* (Paris, 1951), 29.

[18] Over the centuries there has been a chorus of praise and admiration, even rose-tinted sentimentality such as "une oeuvre incomparable de tolérance sincère et charmante." Léonard, "Le Protestantisme français," 154; Gustave Fagniez, *Le Père Joseph et Richelieu*, 2 vols. (Paris, 1894), 1:380; N. Weiss, "Quelques jugements sur l'édit de Nantes," *BSHPF*, 47 (1898).

of juridical chaos. Yet, in spite of its detail, it was *not* a positive, or creative act, comprehensively tailored to achieve defined or agreed objectives, because no such agreed objectives ever existed. To have made the Edict truly workable would have been to legalize what it sought to destroy: namely a formal Huguenot organization which might well have proved durable against the power of the crown. Even so, the Edict left the Huguenots strong enough to be dangerous, because the king was not powerful enough to disarm them. This was not a constructive situation in which to devise ways of establishing the Huguenots securely. Since the basic issues of workability were therefore inevitably evaded, we must recognize—which so far has not been clearly done—that the Edict was nurtured in ambiguity and founded in obfuscation. I shall explain more fully what I mean by that. If there is any truth in its vaunted wisdom, this must be seen in what the king was able to salvage through the preamble to the Edict, its form and its timing. These were Henry's, designed to get it past the *parlements*, to minimize the dangers involved, and to obscure the extent of his unavoidable capitulation. This was no receipe for living happily ever after.

The structure of the Edict was complex and has given rise to much controversy and disagreement. We are dealing in fact with four documents: two sets of articles of 13 April and 2 May respectively—following the pattern of the Edict of Poitiers—plus two royal *brevets,* or acts of grace of 3 and 30 April.[19] The first set of ninety-two articles comprised the religious liberties—heavily weighted in favor of the dangerous nobility—the civil liberties and the judicial safeguards. Many of the arrangements involved, not least in respect of the religious liberties, were extremely complex, difficult to execute and often easy to evade.[20] No aspect of the Edict of Nantes has given rise to greater confusion, which is still *widely* prevalent, than that of the Huguenots' political status. Contrary to what is usually either alleged or implied, the Edict conferred *no* political privileges whatsoever. That it had political *consequences* is incontestable; but that is quite another matter. Political assemblies, and all elements of the Huguenots' activities necessary for making war, including the

---

[19] The Edict of Nantes is printed in various old works, including Élie Benoist, *Histoire de l'édit de Nantes,* 5 vols. (Delft, 1693-95), 1:Recueil, 62-98. It is now most readily available in Mousnier, *L'Assassinat,* 294-334.

[20] This point is stressed and illustrated by Georges Pagès, "Les Paix de religion et l'édit de Nantes," *Revue d'histoire moderne et contemporaine,* n. s., 5 (1936): 410-13.

raising of men and money, were expressly forbidden in article eighty-two.[21] This swept away their so-called "state within the state," illegally reconstituted by the assembly of Sainte-Foy in 1594.[22] Articles of the second group of fifty-six, qualified as secret and particular, explained, interpreted, and covered omissions, exceptions, and contradictions which, in some cases, had been caused by concessions to the Catholic League.   Article thirty-four rather inconspicuously authorized the Calvinist ecclesiastical organization.[23]

The prohibitions of article eighty-two were partially offset by the royal *brevets*. The first obliquely provided for the payment of pastors; the second contained the crucial guarantee clauses. The Huguenots thereby retained about 150 towns. The king was constrained to contribute 180,000 *écus* per annum for the garrisons, and to appoint only acceptable, Protestant governors.[24]

---

[21] Poirson, an early major work, may have been responsible for starting this confusion. He wrote: "L'Édit de Nantes leur laissa deux espèces d'assemblées: les assemblées pour cause de religion ... et les assemblées politiques," citing articles thirty-four of the second set, and eighty-two of the first set—which said the exact opposite. His further observations on the subject of assemblies are garbled and contradictory. *Histoire du règne de Henri IV*, 1:368-69. This error has been widely repeated. For example, according to Perrens, *L'Église et l'état*, 1:135, 148, Henry permitted the Huguenots "en quelque sorte une République dans l'état," including assemblies, which is quite misleading. Léonard, "Le Protestantisme français," 155, 166, is contradictory and also misleading. Assemblies were prohibited, but "par l'édit le Protestantisme devenait . . . un corps politique privilégié. . . ." By 1629, he said, the Huguenots were deprived of political privileges. Pierre Blet, "Le Plan de Richelieu pour la réunion des Protestants," *Gregorianum*, 48 (1967): 101, also said that the Grace of Alais removed "la force politique." A.D. Lublinskaya, *French Absolutism: The Crucial Phase, 1620-1629* (Cambridge, 1968), 156, refers to political privileges having been obtained among many others. W.J. Stankiewicz, *Politics and Religion in Seventeenth-Century France*, 2nd ed. (Westport, Conn., 1976), 63, 112, states that the Edict included the right to hold political assemblies. Pagès, "Les Paix de religion," 407, asserts that the Huguenots later obtained the *right* to hold assemblies with the king's permission.   Faurey, *L'Édit de Nantes*, 31, however, correctly refers to assemblies having been "reconstituées malgré l'interdiction formelle de l'édit." The point has also recently been made by Jean-Pierre Babelon, *Henri IV* (Paris, 1982), 686. Even the very precise historian Mousnier, *L'Assassinat*, 131-32, is not very clear on this matter. He says that the Huguenots received "une organisation politique et une armée," although in principle article eighty-two forbade any political organization. The inference appears to be that permission in the *brevet* to appoint a temporary council of ten at Saumur, and the military guarantees, amounted to a political organization. He later says, p. 139, that general assemblies, in principle held every three years, were in fact held more frequently. This is not so, and the origin of the triennial point is undisclosed. Most recently, Garrisson, *L'Édit de Nantes*, 17, 22, described the privileges of the Edict as political, while her analysis shows that they were not. Even Elisabeth Labrousse, "*Une foi, une loi, un roi?*" 93, said that the Édict "instaurait une sorte d'état dans l'état," whereas it actually sought to abolish the "state" refounded in 1594. That it failed to do so does not affect the juridical point.

[22] Sutherland, "The Edict of Nantes," 200, 214-17; L. Anquez, *Histoire des assemblées politiques des réformés de France* (Paris, 1859), 15ff., 207ff., 228ff., 340ff., 448; Gordon Griffiths, *Representative Government in Western Europe in the Sixteenth Century* (Oxford, 1968), 254-97.

[23] Pagès, "Les Paix de religion," 406, states that the ecclesiastical organization was only implicitly recognized by article forty-three of the second group, whereas it is explicitly recognized in article thirty-four.   The Edict of Poitiers, 1577, had also contained two sets of articles, sixty-four general plus forty-eight so-called secret articles.

[24] Anquez, *Histoire des assemblées*, 160-66, indicates that there were sixty-four garrison towns, five royal free cities, not garrisoned, and seventy-five *places particulières*. The numbers are both approximate

The difference between these documents is juridical and technical, but in executive terms arcane, reflecting the ambiguity and obfuscation to which I have referred. In common parlance, "the Edict" has comprised all four documents—the whole agreement, although only the ninety-two articles were registered by the *parlements*. This verbal convenience was therefore not unassailable. Thus, upon examination, the very Edict itself becomes elusive and debatable.[25] To the Huguenots, the articles depended on the second *brevet*—the guarantee clauses—because they were never convinced that once deprived of the means of defense, they would not soon be deprived of everything else. This indicates a fundamental lack of confidence, not least because the *brevet* was limited to a period of eight years. Thus one could say that the vital aspect to the Edict had only ever been temporary. In 1598 Henry could not have retaken the Huguenots' towns without further prolonged war. Nor could he, in any case, have risked the Huguenots' destruction while he too was gravely menaced by the Papacy and Catholic extremists. Since his armies were not omnipresent he had no alternative—despite their disloyalty—but to suffer the Huguenots to defend themselves.[26] Nevertheless, the *brevet* was clearly derogatory to the power of the crown which must, eventually, recover the towns. Yet, in the face of Huguenot insubordination and a growing miscellany of other problems, the *brevet* was repeatedly extended, finally expiring in 1625.[27] Explicitly deprived of any political structure, the Huguenots' military standing still afforded them political *leverage;* and to be deprived but not disarmed was a dangerous combination. They had not submitted to the king, and herein lay their muscle, as well as the crux of future problems. There remained, therefore, an unresolved issue of authority between the crown and the Huguenots, mainly arising from their need for defense against the Catholics—the vast majority of Henry's subjects whom he had also to conciliate.

---

and variable. Under the Edict of Poitiers, Henry III had undertaken to pay for troops to guard eight *places de sûreté* for six years. The principle was therefore established.

[25] Mousnier, *L'Assassinat*, 128-29, is quite precise about the juridical classification of these documents. In submitting to the *parlement* the articles of 2 May, Henry explained that he had accorded certain further articles that he wished to carry "pareille force et vertu . . . que nostre édit." This would appear to distinguish between the Edict "proper" and other articles, at the same time as giving them equal validity. F.A. Isambert, *Recueil général des anciennes lois françaises*, 29 vols. (Paris, 1829-33), 15:170. There is apparently no record that they were ever registered, 200 n. 1.

[26] Sutherland, "The Edict of Nantes," passim.

[27] There was some controversy in 1605 as to whether the *brevet* had run from 1598 or 1600. It remained uncertain whether it expired in 1606 and 1610 or 1608 and 1612. Anquez, *Histoire des assemblées*, 430, 432.

Far from being hailed as a masterpiece, the Edict was greeted with widespread obloquy.[28] At best, it was regarded as an unavoidable treaty of peace, and a necessary expedient. Even so, it was not merely a Huguenot charter.[29] Article three enjoined the restoration of Catholicism *everywhere* and the return of church property[30] as the general assembly of the clergy had already demanded in 1596. This resulted in a vast resurgence of Catholicism, which might not otherwise have happened, and made it commensurately easier for Catholics to resist the Edict.[31] These Catholic provisions were represented in the preamble as a first step towards a return to one religion ("ne se pouvans tous composer à la fois et en même temps") and it was possible for Henry to inform the pope that the Edict did more for Catholics than for Protestants.[32] If this was diplomacy, or even propaganda, it was also plausible. Catholicism was ostentatiously established as the dominant religion.

The king's intentions were expressed in the preamble, which repays careful study. It is a skillful apology, placing the Edict in its civil-war context. Henry's primary intention was to provide one general law regulating all the differences between those of the two religions, for the establishment of a good and durable peace, so that the worship of god might be at least within one common intention if not yet "en une même forme de religion." The ideal of religious unity was therefore clearly affirmed, albeit without any provocative reference to Rome.[33] Nevertheless, the essential Catholicism of the crown had been sufficiently proclaimed by Henry's own, necessary, problematic abjuration.

---

[28] Yves de La Brière, "Comment fut adopté et accepté l'édit de Nantes," *Etudes*, 99 (1904, suite): 44ff.; Mousnier, *L'Assassinat*, 132, refers to "de véritables explosions de rage"; Frederic J. Baumgartner, "The Catholic Opposition to the Edict of Nantes, 1598-1599," *Bibliothèque d'Humanisme et Renaissance*, 40 (1978): 525-36.

[29] Tayeneaux, *Le Catholicisme*, 1:24, states, precisely, that it *was* a Huguenot charter, and Perrens, *L'Église et l'état*, 1:135, that it was an excessive charter setting them up as they wished to be. They showed no signs of satisfaction.

[30] According to Perrens, *L'Église et l'état*, 1:136, Catholicism was restored to one hundred cities and 1,000 parishes—approximately, no doubt. The retention of church property by those who had acquired it was undoubtedly one reason for continued resistance.

[31] Where and when the Huguenots were strong, they also resisted the Catholic restitution. See, for instance, Robert Sauzet, *Contre réforme et réforme catholique en Bas-Languedoc. Le Diocèse de Nîmes au XVIIe siècle* (Paris, 1979), 192, 195, 199.

[32] Mousnier, *L'Assassinat*, 132-34.

[33] This suggests a temporary, if not a brief arrangement.

Much could be said on the allied subject of Catholic pressure of the king. Henry had been excommunicated as a heretic in 1585 and declared inapt. After the Edict the angry and offended pope threatened him a second time with excommunication. This would have comprised his deposition and released all Catholics from the duty of obedience.[34] Thus one need not be over subtle about the preamble to the Edict. Henry was striving to unite and reconcile, and to purchase time. But the close association of religion and justice made the protection of a minority religion incredibly difficult. That no government can achieve what the courts will not enforce is a very ancient and a very modern problem of authority. While Henry wished the Huguenots to rely on the courts, they saw their only hope in the sovereign authority of the crown. Yet, paradoxically, they defied and diminished that saving authority because it was insufficient to avert the Catholics' hostility. This was a destructive course.

It has already been stated that the Edict did not fundamentally alter the relations between the crown and the Huguenots. The conflicts from which the Edict had arisen continued without interruption in respect of its contested execution. The new phase of conflict was not essentially about the provisions of the Edict—although these were instantly transgressed and constantly disputed—but about procedures, ways and means. This was a problem of authority, arising from inherent contradictions and inadequacies—those ambiguities and obfuscations—which themselves derived from the same problem of authority and divergence of interest between the crown and the Huguenots; they were trapped together in a maze with no discernible exit. This continuing conflict quickly focused on the existence and status of the Huguenots as a corporate body.[35]

We have seen that article eighty-two explicitly destroyed the Huguenots as a corporate body in the political sense. It is doubtful, however, if the problem was ever consciously formulated; it would in any case have been too hot to handle. Royal acceptance of Protestants envisaged individuals and churches. But as early as 1560, they had become a political party, and after the massacre of St. Bartholomew in 1572, they organized their so-called "state" and became a corporate body. That was dis-

---

[34] Babelon, *Henri IV,* part 2, chaps. 1, 9; 692ff.; Perrens, *L'Église et l'état,* 1:137ff.; John Viénot, *Histoire de la réforme française de l'édit de Nantes à sa révocation,* 2 vols. (Paris, 1934), 1:6ff., 60; Mousnier, *L'Assassinat,* 122-66.

[35] This struggle can be followed in Anquez, *Histoire des assemblées,* 172ff.

solved with Henry's accession in 1589, illegally renewed in 1594, and dissolved again by the Edict in 1598. The second *brevet*, however, with its guarantee clauses, went either too far, or not far enough. It implicitly recognized, *de facto*, that corporate existence which the Edict—article eighty-two—abolished *de jure*. The degree of independence, control and self-defense implied by the guarantees required, in practice, some complementary organization through which to operate, and this produced an untenable contradiction in the terms of the Edict. There was also the problem of the prohibition against the raising of men and money, without which a military function was impossible.[36] The *brevet* addressed itself to the maintenance of the hostage towns in marvellously unrevealing terms. In theory these were transient problems which would expire with the *brevet* and the full restoration of royal authority. In practice the basic issues were evaded. The Huguenots could not be made only temporarily secure; thus they were allowed, yet not allowed, to be. This can be shown by their immediate relations with the king.

The *brevet* had authorized the assembly of Châtellerault to appoint a committee of ten to remain at Saumur until the registration of the Edict.[37] Its promulgation did not, however, terminate the assembly—which had opened on 16 June 1597 during the royal siege of Amiens. Its insubordinate prolongation, in order to supervise the execution of an Edict expressly prohibiting assemblies, was a truly astonishing paradox. In order to be rid of this defiant assembly Henry consented to accept one or two deputies, to be resident at court, to take charge of Huguenot affairs. He further authorized a new assembly at Sainte-Foy in October 1601 to elect this *députation générale*.[38] Henry kept control of the new assembly—which is what he was trying to do—only to the extent that it was small and brief; but it was *not* innocuous. Foreseeing future difficulties, members seized their immediate opportunity to resuscitate the illegal, political organization. It was skillfully blended with their ecclesiastical institutions so that, in case of need, the churches could serve political purposes, con-

---

[36] Article eighty-two.

[37] The Edict was not submitted to the *parlement* until after the departure of the legate in September 1598, and then the king had to accept amendments which the Huguenots in turn resisted. It was registered in Paris on 25 February 1599; Grenoble, 27 September 1599; Dijon, 12 January 1600; Toulouse, 19 January 1600; Bordeaux, 1600; Aix and Rennes, 11 and 23 August 1600; Rouen, 1609. Anquez, *Histoire des assemblées*, 174-83, 187-91; Mousnier, *L'Assassinat*, 135. Mousnier also prints Henry's masterly discours au parlement, 7 January 1599, 334-37.

[38] Anquez, *Histoire des assemblées*, 186. The *députation générale* proved to be lasting. Drion, *Histoire chronologique*, 2:161, refers to a single deputy in May 1681.

trary to the tenor of the Edict. They also sought to squeeze a maximum advantage from the concession of court deputies. They drafted a *règlement* providing for the election, by a general assembly or a national synod, of two deputies to serve for one year only. Their far-reaching duties were defined, and they were to report to the next general assembly which would elect their successors.[39] This was a bid for annual general assemblies, as well as for control of the court deputies. These transactions revealed that illegal provincial assemblies had never been dissolved.[40] The Edict was already severely breached by the Huguenots themselves.

Lacking a prince, or any supreme, co-ordinating leadership, the Huguenots faced a serious problem of communication. This would become desperate if the king succeeded in breaking the chain of general assemblies in which each provided for the next. Consequently, those at Sainte-Foy took measures to set up a small council of at least five members in each Huguenot province, for general purposes of liaison and to be the principal channels of communication for the new court deputies.[41] For this reason the councils, or standing committees, were well and inconspicuously intermingled with the ecclesiastical organization. If necessary, they could also circumvent the illegality of the provincial assemblies. These illegal provisions of Sainte-Foy illustrate the Huguenots' conception of themselves as a nationwide, corporate body, expressing and governing itself through a political hierarchy, albeit vitiated, which both paralleled and mingled with their Presbyterian church structure. This was something the king could neither suppress nor afford to ignore.

Proceeding from these events, the conflict centered on two principal issues: general assemblies and the court deputies. The king—Henry IV and Louis XIII after him—contested the frequency, duration, size, composition and competence of the Huguenot assemblies, which they were unable to prevent and were constrained either to authorize, to endure or to legalize. For their part, the assemblies made a tenacious and aggressive stand for the redress of grievances before dispersal. They were well aware that their interminable complaints, however genuine, were seldom matters of contention between themselves and the crown, but mainly stemmed from the admin-

---

[39] Anquez, *Histoire des assemblées*, 207-212.

[40] Ibid., 183, 209.

[41] Ibid., 209-210.

istrative limitations of royal power. The second main contention centered on the selection, length of service and accountability of the court deputies. In this connection, as we have already seen, the assemblies adopted a number of ploys for attempting to afflict the king with continuous assemblies which represented and could mobilize the provincial power of the Huguenots. Through assemblies they could act; without them, they were decapitated.

While their attitude was one of confrontation, they did also face genuine and serious difficulties deriving from the origins and nature of the Edict—its ambiguities and obfuscations. To propose and accept the court deputies was to admit the Huguenots' need for communication and dialogue with the crown. By implication and extension, Henry had also sanctioned their election—or selection—and recognized their necessary relations with those whom they served and represented. Yet there was no specified, *legal* channel of communication or machinery behind the deputies through which to operate. In these circumstances they could only liaise with illegal bodies, or work through the organization of the churches. How were they to determine what was legal and what was not—if indeed this bothered them? While it is easy to differentiate, for instance, between doctrine and elections, or penance and war, it was not simple to distinguish either between political and ecclesiastical business or, within a Presbyterian church structure, between secular and ecclesiastical personnel. To allow the Huguenots their churches while attempting to isolate them from non-ecclesiastical matters was an unrealistic, Catholic attitude, and a practical impossibility, which was therefore never achieved.

Thus, in spite of the intransigence of successive assemblies, there was a genuine sense in which they could be said to be necessary. Yet, like the deputies, they too had to be elected somehow, which therefore presupposed some sort of provincial machinery, such as the Edict had abolished but not actually destroyed. This could, in theory, be resolved by the terms of each commission, but not without risks and undesirable precedents. For the king to authorize an assembly, or to regularize an illegal one, was to postulate a head without a body, or to recognize the apex of an illegal organization, infringing the unworkable Edict. It is possible that the crown might have been induced to accept the principle of periodic assemblies, at least for the election of deputies and the presentation of a single *cahier*, or remonstrance, had they consented to be governed by narrow procedural rules and limitations.[42] But "they" comprised not only the assemblies themselves, whose conduct could never be pre-empted, but also those unpredictable communities from which they sprang. In practice, the size, composition and conduct of assemblies tended to provoke a dangerous Catholic reaction, and it must be constantly remembered that the king's handling of the Huguenots—whether Henry IV or Louis XIII—was always in a context of danger.[43]

Consequently these dilemmas were evaded; indeed, there is no evidence that they were ever analyzed. So the Huguenots repeatedly exploited the existence of the *députation générale* to extort assemblies, while the crown sustained the principle that assemblies were illegal, and that the king should control the choice, tenure and service of the deputies.[44] Yet it failed to find any alternative means of electing them which did not also undermine the Edict.[45] Thus both the crown and the Huguenots found themselves in an untenable position. Lack of confidence on both sides produced a continuous state of friction, in which the Huguenots maintained an insubordinate attitude. Henry condemned the continued existence of illegal provincial assemblies in 1606 but, faced with a serious rebellion by the duc de Bouillon, himself a Protestant, he could not contemplate recovering the hostage towns, whether by diplomacy or war. He was therefore forced to renew the *brevet* for another four years.[46] This had the effect of extending the problem of the towns into the following reign. The fact that Henry had neither been able to control the Huguenots, nor to impose his will,[47]

---

[42] See, for example, the way in which Henry sought to control the assembly of Châtellerault, May 1605, which, he declared, was the last he would authorize. Anquez, *Histoire des assemblées*, 212-13. He was, however, obliged to authorize another at Jargeau in October 1608.

[43] The assembly of Châtellerault, 16 June 1597 (reconvened at Saumur, November 1599-31 May 1601) partially coincided with the Biron conspiracy. Another assembly of Châtellerault in 1605 occurred in the same year as the Bouillon conspiracy. Under Louis XIII the assembly of Grenoble, July 1615, which removed to Nîmes and La Rochelle, coincided with Condé's second rebellion and supported him.

[44] Marie de Medici declared all assemblies illegal, not because they had previously been lawful but because illegal provincial assemblies were widespread. Benoist, *Histoire de l'édit de Nantes*, 2:Recueil, 25-27, 24 April 1612, déclaration sur les assemblées, which referred to article eighty-two of the Edict of Nantes and the *ordonnance* of 1606. They were again declared illegal on 11 July 1612, in 1617, 1618 and by the Peace of Montpellier, 1622. Ibid., 45-47; Anquez, *Histoire des assemblées*, 255.

[45] In 1603, to avoid an assembly, Henry got the synod of Gap to authorize the existing deputies to act, breaching the Edict by using an ecclesiastical body for a political purpose.

[46] Benoist, *Histoire de l'édit de Nantes*, 2:Recueil, 26, the *ordonnance* of 16 March 1606 declaring assemblies to be illegal; 4 August 1605, Anquez, *Histoire des assemblées*, 430.

[47] This was not recognized by Taveneaux, *Le Catholicisme*, 1:24, who sees the Edict as having been successful on account of the restoration of monarchical power. This hardly accounts for the hostage towns; if anything it was the restoration of monarchical power which destroyed the Edict.

rendered them on the one hand more dangerous and, on the other, more vulnerable under a weaker government. When Henry was murdered in May 1610, they become aware of how much they had lost.[48]

Henry himself foresaw that relations between the crown and the Huguenots were likely to degenerate—one might interpolate especially under a regency—in which case their status and the stability of the Edict must be jeopardized. The Huguenots, he said, had abused his good will (bonté) believing that he would never turn against them. That, he cheerfully acknowledged, was true.[49] Nevertheless their conduct, he predicted, would later spell their ruin because they would continue to behave towards his son as they had treated him and, not sharing his father's sentiments, Louis would not stand for it.[50] If things worked out a little differently, it is true that they were largely the architects of their own destruction.

In Louis's reign the Huguenot opposition was more explicitly directed against the crown, upon whose authority they still depended. If Louis was not necessarily subjected to stronger Catholic pressures than Henry IV, he was himself more closely identified with Catholics than his father could ever have been. Furthermore, power and influence passed to extremist opponents of the Edict while Louis was still too young to rule alone. The Catholic ethos of his reign was undeniable, under the influence of powerful Counter Reformation forces, and there were those who called for a crusade, seeking opportunities to ruin the Huguenots.[51] Contrary to prevalent assumptions, there is no evidence that this was what Louis had in mind. In fact his early attitudes, before 1629, are difficult to ascertain, never having been put to the test. During this period, he was to renew the Edict at least fifteen times, and never persecuted heretics. But after his own assumption of power, following a dramatic coup d'état in 1617, he was adamant that he would not tolerate rebellion which, if undesirable, at least afforded him the opportunity to assert his own authority. It was

---

[48] The murder of Henry IV remains largely mysterious, but the deeply suspicious circumstances suggest an ultra-Catholic, pro-Spanish plot, relating to foreign policy.

[49] Henry employed a large number of Protestants, partly through the influence and work of Sully. They were, also, less dangerous than Catholics to the king himself.

[50] Anquez, Histoire des assemblées, 391, quoting the memoirs of Fontenay-Mareuil.

[51] Viénot, Histoire de la réforme, 1:131ff.; Victor-L. Tapié, France in the Age of Louis XIII and Richelieu (Cambridge, 1984), part 1, chap. 3.

also to his ultimate advantage that the suppression of rebellion could be interpreted by the clergy, and the Catholics of his entourage, as meeting their demands for action against the heretics. At the same time, by 1622 their own internal collapse as a corporate body, and the steady detachment of the provincial nobility, altered the nature of the Huguenot problem and of the Huguenots as a collectivity.

Under Marie de Medici as regent, and Louis XIII after her, problems intrinsic to the Edict continued to focus on the existence of the Huguenots as a corporate body.[52] Like Henry IV, they both experienced strictly similar conflicts with assemblies, authorized and unauthorized, and over the extension of the *brevet* and the election and function of the deputies.[53] The illegal political organization was strengthened by the assembly of Saumur in 1611, and given a complete military structure—at least on paper—by the illegal assembly of La Rochelle in 1621.[54]

Henry IV had succeeded in isolating the Huguenots from the noble rebellions.[55] But, in 1615, under the regency,[56] some of the Huguenots turned once again to the nobility in arms and began to make general, political demands, which had nothing to do with either their status or the Edict.[57] Furthermore, they became partly responsible for the downfall of the regency government in 1616. Thus, when Louis himself asssumed power in 1617, Huguenot activists had for seven years been disobedient, demanding and rebellious. It could therefore be argued that, unlike his father, Louis owed them nothing. He appears, however, to have perceived their fragmentation, and chose to distinguish between loyal heretics and Huguenot rebels.[58] Since he was no

---

[52] The assembly of Saumur in 1611 also demanded the original, unmodified Edict that had already been demanded and refused in 1601 and 1602. Benoist, *Histoire de l'édit de Nantes*, 2:Recueil, 9.

[53] Anquez, *Histoire des assemblées*, 226ff.; Anquez, *Un Nouveau chapitre de l'histoire politique des réformés de France, 1621-1626* (Paris, 1865), passim; for an analysis of the *cahiers* topic by topic from 1601-1622, see Anquez, *Un Nouveau chapitre*, 391ff. David Parker, *La Rochelle and the French Monarchy* (London, 1980), 200-206, has established a list of assemblies, but without indicating whether they were authorized, illegal, legalized or repudiated.

[54] Benoist, *Histoire de l'édit de Nantes*, 2:Recueil, 5-9, règlement général . . . des églises réformées, 29 August 1611; Anquez, *Histoire des assemblées*, 228-43, 340-42, 10 May 1621, l'ordre et règlement général de milice et de finances.

[55] The Biron conspiracy, 1601-1602; the Auvergne conspiracy, 1604; the Bouillon conspiracy, 1605-1606.

[56] Marie de Medici, mother of Louis XIII, regent *de jure* 1610-14, *de facto* 1614-17.

[57] Anquez, *Histoire des assemblées*, 267-68.

[58] See for example, Benoist, *Histoire de l'édit de Nantes*, 2:Recueil, 35-38 (10 November 1615, declara-

more able than any other monarch to exterminate heresy, this was a wise and effective *via media*.

The hostilities which occurred in Louis's reign, and which enabled him to tackle the problem of the hostage towns, developed initially from another issue of authority: the status of the Béarn, a Bourbon patrimonial territory.[59] The restoration of Catholicism and church property in Béarn had been one of the conditions of Henry IV's papal absolution in 1595.[60] Since that territory was excluded from the Edict of Nantes, this matter was regarded by the Catholics as unfinished business, and Louis inherited a conciliar decision to complete it. Aged sixteen, and surrounded by experienced Catholic politicians, he issued an edict of restitution in June 1617 which, however, the Béarnais steadily ignored.[61] Consequently, after suppressing a rebellion led by his mother and supported by the Huguenots, Louis marched on from Poitou into Béarn in October 1620. There he enforced the edict relating to Béarn and annexed the territory to the crown. If the conduct of the soldiery was not entirely genteel, this was still an act of authority, and not of persecution or of war.[62] The new régime resembled that of Nantes, and there is no evidence that Louis intended any subsequent action against the Huguenots. They had, however, espoused the cause of Béarn—which they were shortly to abandon—and this afforded a convenient pretext for those among them who positively sought the resumption of war. So it was that Louis's authority was directly defied by a new sort of illegal and revolutionary assembly at La Rochelle, which declared itself sovereign, seized direction of Huguenot affairs, organized the military structure and called out several southern provinces in rebellion.[63]

---

tion on the taking up of arms), 53-55 (24 April 1621, declaration in favor of obedient Protestants), 56-58 (7 June 1621, declaration against rebellious Protestants, protecting the obedient).

[59] Anquez, *Histoire des assemblées*, 298-311, 327-29.

[60] Mousnier, *L'Assassinat*, 99-100, sets out the terms of the papal absolution.

[61] 25 June 1617. Anquez, *Histoire des assemblées*, 309; 10 November 1617, the Béarnais edict rejecting that of the king.

[62] Before entering Béarn, Louis ordered the *parlement* to register the edict of 1617 and offered a pardon for past disobedience. Anquez, *Histoire des assemblées*, 327; Tapié, *France in the Age of Louis XIII*, 116-19.

[63] Anquez, *Histoire des assemblées*, 331-53. The provinces were Bas-Languedoc, Cévennes, Vivarais, and Dauphiné.

The deeper truth of this matter is still obscure. In propaganda and polemics the Protestant resistance of Béarn was linked with the Bohemian rebellion of 1618 which, in terms of the old cliché, is said to have sparked off the Thirty Years' War. There doubtless was some generalized fear that the government meant to exploit the involvement of Protestant powers in Germany to destroy the Huguenots in France. The logic is tenuous, but the matter emotive and not unimportant. The English parliament of 1621 was prepared to support James I in a war for the cause of religion, which included not only the Calvinist Rhine Palatinate, but also the Huguenots as well.[64] That the Huguenots' religious liberties were never once endangered was either unknown, disbelieved, or disregarded for reasons of policy. Certainly from 1621-29 the Huguenot saga cannot be isolated from the kaleidoscopic complications of European diplomacy and war, which once again turned the Huguenots into an exploitable force.[65] This was all the more significant since one of their hostage towns was the independent citadel of La Rochelle, the only port on the Atlantic coast capable of harboring a royal fleet; and ships were to be a priority of Cardinal Richelieu, who came to power in August 1624.[66] This is the direction in which we must look for explanations of the otherwise largely inexplicable. No one, however, has so far admitted that the Huguenot cause, or the cause of religion—were they, or were they not the same—becomes increasingly difficult to identify. Allegedly, for the nobles, it had something to do with the retention of church property and, for the towns, the preservation of fiscal privileges.[67]

Louis did not take the field in 1621 without first warning the assembly of La Rochelle, and offering protection to the obedient. The issue was not religion, but rebellion and authority. His campaigns of 1621 and 1622 met with relatively little resistance—because the interests of the towns lay with the king—and brought the re-

---

[64] S. L. Adams, "The Road to La Rochelle: English Foreign Policy and the Huguenots 1610-1629," *Proceedings of the Huguenot Society of London*, 22 (5) (1975): 422-23; Tapié, *France in the Age of Louis XIII*, 105-106, discusses propaganda about Protestant intentions.

[65] As early as 1612 James I had issued a declaration offering to protect the Huguenots, and the duc de Bouillon was highly connected in European Protestant circles. Adams, "The Road to La Rochelle," 418 and passim.

[66] On the whole question of La Rochelle, see Parker, *La Rochelle and the French Monarchy*.

[67] Lublinskaya, *French Absolutism*, 214-15. The non-restoration of church property was, of course, contrary to the Edict.

covery of roughly half the hostage towns.[68] The antics of the assembly and the king's increasing authority also hastened the defection of the leading nobility, without whom the Huguenots could not wage war. Only the duc de Rohan and his brother Soubise persisted in a changing and a losing "cause."[69] By the summer of 1622, the crown was for the first time in a relatively strong position. Thus the Peace of Montpellier, 19 October 1622, is interesting for the light which it throws on the attitude of the crown to the Edict of Nantes, which was clarified, and on the problem of the Huguenots as a corporate body.[70]

Louis had successfully asserted his authority, but it was not yet complete. The Huguenots still held some seventy towns for which the *brevet* was confirmed up to 1625—the already existing terminal date.[71] Louis renewed all the clauses relating to civil and religious liberties, property and offices. But every variety of assembly—exhaustively specified—was categorically forbidden; so also was the use of ecclesiastical bodies for political purposes. While this was the obvious meaning of the Edict of Nantes, the point had not previously been emphasized.[72] Louis also confirmed the *députation générale,* and conceded that he *might* authorize a triennial assembly (not that he would) for the replacement of the deputies and the submission of a single *cahier*, his replies to be conveyed to the deputies, not to the assembly. It was ironic that this tardy acceptance of the need for assemblies—or anyway the impossibility of avoiding them—should have coincided with the Huguenots' collapse as a corporate body and the end, as it transpired, of general assemblies; for nothing more was heard of the assembly of La Rochelle or their radical experiment.[73]

---

[68] Louis was halted by Montauban, August-November 1621, and by Montpellier, September-October 1622; both sieges failed.

[69] Anquez, *Histoire des assemblées*, 349-50, 355-56; Anquez, *Un Nouveau chapitre*, 27-34; Viénot, *Histoire de la réforme*, 1:198-200; Schybergson, "Le duc de Rohan," 49-51.

[70] Anquez, *Histoire des assemblées*, 385-89, 438-42; Benoist, *Histoire de l'édit de Nantes*, 2:Recueil, 60-62, 19 October 1622, déclaration sur la paix.

[71] Provision for the demolition of fortifications and the retention of certain hostage towns were contained in subsequent *brevets* of 24 and 25 October 1622. Anquez, *Un Nouveau chapitre*, 19-21.

[72] This clause in the Peace of Montpellier has given rise to a widespread supposition that assemblies had previously been legal.

[73] Anquez, *Un Nouveau chapitre*, 25-27.

This recognition was, however, more an attempt to clarify and impose the royal authority than to solve a problem intrinsic to the Edict. Thus the peace still neglected to provide for any legal means by which even an authorized assembly could be elected. Similarly, there was no legal body, apart from the churches, from which the contents of the *cahiers* could originate, or to which the deputies could transmit the answers.[74] Marie de Medici had been constrained, as a concession, to recognize the provincial councils organized in 1601, but these were now expressly prohibited.[75] Thus, like the remaining hostage towns, the court deputies survived in a vacuum.

After the Peace of Montpellier in 1622, the Huguenot story had little to do with the Edict of Nantes, but primarily centered on a struggle for the control of La Rochelle, within the context of the continental war.[76] Historians still dispute the Huguenot policy of Cardinal Richelieu, though it hardly seems mysterious.[77] It is certain that, from 1624, his preoccupations were the retention of power and the defense of French interests in north Italy. If, indeed, he wanted further Huguenot campaigns—which has rather been assumed than demonstrated—he cannot have wanted them when they occurred in 1624-26 and 1627-29, endangering the foreign policy for which he needed domestic peace.[78]

It is not necessary to venture into the diplomatic tangle behind the first of these two risings at La Rochelle, during which Soubise took flight to England. The independence of La Rochelle was largely destroyed by the peace of that name in February

---

[74] From 1623 the crown held tighter control over religious assemblies, which required permission and the attendance of a royal official. Benoist, *Histoire de l'édit de Nantes*, 2:Recueil, 73-75, 17 April 1623.

[75] 1613; Anquez, *Histoire des assemblées*, 261.

[76] Probably the best general account from the Huguenot point of view is in Anquez, *Un Nouveau chapitre*, but it ends in 1626.

[77] Clearly, in a religious sense, Richelieu deprecated heresy. Restrictive measures against the Huguenots occurred during the rest of his ministry and the reign of Louis XIII. Drion, *Histoire chronologique*, 2:8ff.; Blet, "Le Plan de Richelieu," 100-129; "Mémoire adressée à Richelieu par le ministre Philippe Codur," *BHSPF*, 39 (1890), a plan to break up the Protestant ecclesiastical organization and reunite the Huguenots to the Catholic Church. The project was revived in 1645. Faurey, *L'Édit de Nantes*, 32; Fagniez, *Le Père Joseph*, 385, 428-35. Fagniez even suggests that Richelieu would not have been averse from a patriarchate, not unlike the Cardinal of Lorraine in 1561.

[78] The Huguenots were capable of realizing that Richelieu needed peace. Besides, in January or February 1625, he offered to pardon Rohan and Soubise, planning to employ Rohan in north Italy and Soubise against Genoa. This indicates that Richelieu was not straining to complete the destruction of the Huguenots in battle. Anquez, *Un Nouveau chapitre*, 130-31; Benoist, *Histoire de l'édit de Nantes*, 2:Recueil, 77, 25 January 1626, declaration against Soubise and offer of pardon.

1626,[79] and it is at least questionable whether the government need, for its own objectives, have taken further action. In the event, the famous siege was precipitated by another rebellion in 1627, mainly due to the desire of the Huguenots for their English alliance and to the collapse of Anglo-French relations.[80] As, in both cases, the rebellious initiative had lain with the Huguenots, it is an absurdity to credit or discredit their final overthrow to the skill or the villainy of Richelieu, as has commonly been the case.

Richelieu, however, did take part both in the dramatic siege of La Rochelle and in the last, successful campaign in Languedoc against the duc de Rohan. It is widely received opinion that the Grace of Alais in June 1629 was for him a triumph of wisdom and of moderation.[81] But, for reasons of home and foreign policy, neither in 1626 nor in 1629 could Richelieu possibly have risked the formal ruination of the Huguenots. The king, for his part, was morally committed to an Edict he had so many times renewed, and to the obedient majority of Protestants he had promised to protect. For a royal declaration, in the form of an edict, there was nothing to negotiate, and there were few decisions to be made. Its inevitable contents were obvious to all concerned. Rohan and Soubise were pardoned and the civil and religious clauses of the Edict were yet again confirmed. Assemblies, as always, were illegal; the *brevet* had finally expired, and there was no further question of hostage towns. The long confrontation was over, and the ideal of Catholic unity was clearly reaffirmed.[82] This might be construed as a warning to the Huguenots: they were now no more than heretics in a Catholic world which resented their juridical equality. For thirty years they had flouted the Edict, claiming more than it accorded. Now their corporate existence was extinguished and their defenses destroyed, but quite as much by time and their own failings as by any action of the crown.

---

[79] Anquez, *Un Nouveau chapitre*, 300; Benoist, *Histoire de l'édit de Nantes*, 2:Recueil, 80-81, 11 February 1626. England's guarantee of the peace is in Benoist, *Histoire de l'édit de Nantes*, 2:Recueil, 81, 6 April 1626.

[80] Adams, "The Road to La Rochelle," 425. An Anglo-French alliance was concluded in May 1625. A declaration of 5 August 1627 refers to the failure of the recent—marriage—treaty with England, her assault on the Ile de Ré, assistance to Soubise and attempts to raise further Protestant rebellion. All this, it was claimed, had nothing to do with religion and Soubise was declared a rebel and destituted. Benoist, *Histoire de l'édit de Nantes*, 2:Recueil, 87-90. Geoffrey Parker, *The Thirty Years' War* (London, 1984), 71-81.

[81] Benoist, *Histoire de l'édit de Nantes*, 2:Recueil, 92-98, 27 June 1629, Grace of Alais, and July 1629, Edict of Nîmes; Drion, *Histoire chronologique*, 2:5-6.

[82] Article two: "nous ne pouvons que nous ne désirons leur conversion."

UNDERSTANDING THE REVOCATION OF THE EDICT OF NANTES FROM THE PERSPECTIVE OF THE FRENCH COURT*

Elisabeth Labrousse

Few political decisions have roused historians to such a swift condemnation, indeed such a unanimous censure as the Revocation of the Edict of Nantes, signed at Fontainebleau on 17 October 1685. At the time, however, the Revocation was greeted in France with widespread and unsolicited enthusiasm. Its partial failure—creating as it did more problems than it solved—caused disappointment and slowly led the public to question its legitimacy. Ensuing generations perceived the Edict of Fontainebleau and the anti-Protestant policies which it consecrated as an enormous error and a serious political misjudgment. Such an attitude is too well-known to merit consideration here.

However, a deeper analysis, if attempted, might yield a firmer understanding of the nature of the major political error embodied in the Revocation and the policies of the preceding years. For, from 1660, the application of the Edict of Nantes was undermined by a series of measures at growing variance with its initial provisions. It is necessary, then, to make a clear distinction between the *objective* and the *object* of the Edict of Revocation. The *object* was religious. It abolished the public practice of the *R.P.R.*[1] throughout the kingdom of France, although Alsace was quickly an exception to the rule. It restored Catholicism to its exclusive monopoly, again with the exception of Alsace, where Lutheranism was permitted, and it suppressed—or was supposed to suppress—those pockets of religious non-conformity to be found among the French people. This object expresses an aspiration common to the age. England is an eloquent example of a nation that tried to suppress its religious dissidents before finally coming to terms with them.

---

* Translated by Ruth Whelan. By court I mean not simply the milieu of Versailles, but the government, the authorities, those with power, beginning with, of course, the king.

[1] "Religion prétendue réformée," that is, "self-styled reformed religion," the legal term in France that was somewhat disparaging.

49

Now the ultimate *objective* of the Revocation—as distinct from the means, the authoritarian imposition of religious uniformity—seems to have been dictated by a certain conception of the politics of Reason of State. In other words, the Revocation attempted to abolish a *religious* heresy, because it was thought to harbor a *political* heresy: the Reformed religion was seen as a potential threat to monarchy.

Did the unbridled utilitarianism of the Revocation, whose measures express an indifference to the rights of the underdog, serve the interests of the Gallican Church as enunciated by its clergy? Such is the thesis of a historiographical tradition started by Élie Benoist's precocious history of the Edict of Nantes (1693-94) and continued by authors of more or less anti-clerical tendencies.[2] Or did this utilitarianism attempt first and foremost to serve interests of state summed up in the old adage: *cuius regio, eius religio?*[3]

The proposed dilemma is, of course, simplistic. For, the two kinds of motive evidently interacted. But I wish to concentrate here only on the temporal and utilitarian motives which led Versailles to the Revocation, without taking into account the rhetorical embellishments which sought to present the measures as so much Christian piety and charity—in other words as in keeping with the proprieties and with honor. These utilitarian motivations abound in anti-Protestant controversy and it is easy to collect them, even when they appear only in the background.

Moreover, the evidence seems to indicate that technical or theological controversy only affected a small catchment of readers. The most dangerous works for the French Reformed churches were, on the one hand, writings of a juridical nature, which accumulated precedents and suggested a thousand ingenious and devious ways to harass the Huguenots. On the other, an insidious controversy had infiltrated historical writings destined for a general readership. Such works took the form of accounts of recent sixteenth- and early seventeenth-century history and channelled a venomous anti-Protestant ideology through their tendentious and partial narratives of the recent past. Maimbourg[4] was not alone in this *genre* and works of this kind

---

[2] Such as Henri Martin or Ernest Lavisse, not to say Jules Michelet.

[3] Or "whose the region, his the religion." In France it could also be expressed as "Une foi, une loi, un roi" ("one faith, one law, one king")—in any given territory, one religion only.

[4] Louis Maimbourg (1610-86), for many years a Jesuit, wrote many popular history books, among

certainly prepared public opinion to congratulate the court on its anti-Protestant policies.

A. The essentialist nature of the seventeenth-century mind is well-known among specialists. It was a mind peopled with universal types, for example the miser or the braggart. Now, among these types figured what might be called the Platonic Idea of the Protestant, that is to say, a troublemaker, a disturber of the peace, a rebel, or at least potentially so. The history of France in particular lent itself to this kind of imagery, although with apparent impartiality; when they came to the Wars of Religion, writers vituperated both Huguenots and *Ligueurs*—those sixteenth-century Catholics, dead set against any concession to Protestants. However, and here is the nub of the problem, the descendants of the *Ligueurs* had become unrecognizable and thus invisible. They were only to be found among some of the *dévots*, in whom the earlier political militancy had discovered other outlets. On the other hand, the Huguenots were still there and could be identified with their ancestors, albeit unfairly. For, these seventeenth-century *réformés* differed considerably from their sixteenth-century counterparts, if only in their utter devotion to the divine right of the absolutist king. While the nobility bathed in the reflected glory of the exploits of their forbears, the Huguenots carried the reflected blame of the recourse to arms and the uprisings of the sixteenth and early seventeenth centuries—a reputation which compromised them to a man. The image of the Protestant was, therefore, both hateful and dangerous, given the inveterate propensity to rebellion attributed to him by public opinion. The image was, then, not primarily based on religious differences, although Protestantism was thought to lead to political insubordination.

B. The weak position of the Huguenots[5] and their loyalism to the monarch during the *Fronde*—a loyalism publicly acknowledged in Mazarin's celebrated "Déclaration royale" of 1652—might have mitigated the unfortunate collective image we have just mentioned. But events abroad made it impossible. Not alone were the United Provinces and the Swiss Cantons republics; all of a sudden Protestant England joined the ranks. The Revolution in England prepared the ground for the Revocation inas-

---

them histories of Lutheranism and Calvinism. See Elisabeth Israels Perry, *From Theology to History: French Religious Controversy and the Revocation of the Edict of Nantes* (The Hague, 1973).

[5] They were no more than 6 percent of the total population of the kingdom.

much as Protestant subjects at that time had the audacity to bring their legitimate monarch to trial and a trial ending in a capital sentence (February 1649).[6] Moreover, the regicide was followed by the setting up of a Commonwealth. Was this not proof positive that Protestantism was inseparable from a "republican" spirit, that is to say, from a mentality most unwelcome in a monarchy?

The divide between the Church of England—backbone of the royalist party and teaching a *via media* between Rome and Geneva—and the Reformed Churches of France was common knowledge in Paris given that the English royalists present at the court of Queen Marie-Henriette,[7] in exile at Saint-Germain, were completely unsympathetic to the Huguenots, whom they quite rightly regarded as the counterpart of the much hated Presbyterians. For, despite the fact that they had to be ousted from the Commons before the parliamentary party could become more radical, the Presbyterians had been nonetheless the instigators of Charles I's difficulties. Moreover, if the English at Saint-Germain had frequented the Reformed church at Charenton, they would have come across the *de facto* emissaries of the English parliament and later Cromwell's ambassadors!

The confusion and complexity of the different religious tendencies across the Channel completely escaped the French, who simply condemned the English rebels *en bloc*, neglecting to distinguish the Presbyterians—those moderate monarchists—from the Independents or the Sectaries. That is to say, they confused the moderate royalists with a denomination whose congregationalist ecclesiology the French Protestants hated and had explicitly condemned at the national synod of Charenton in 1644. Moreover, both persuasions were lumped together with a variety of sectarian and illuminist groups quite alien to the Huguenots.

French *réformé* writers were loud in their condemnation of the Independents and the sectarian movements but they were even more eloquent in their pathetic insistence on their respect for the Anglicans. Their efforts were doomed to failure because the English refugees in France snubbed them haughtily and rejected their advances. To crown it all, Cromwell paraded himself as the official protector of continental

---

[6] This date is New Style, used on the continent. England used Old Style, ten days behind the continent.

[7] This daughter of Henry IV of France had been married to Charles I of England and allowed to stay Roman Catholic. She had a certain influence on her husband, which proved disastrous to him.

Protestants. Such protection was useful to the Vaudois in Piedmont, harassed once again in 1655 by the Duke of Savoy: for Mazarin's desire for Cromwell's support against Spain was instrumental in persuading the Duke to stop the persecution. But any association with Cromwell was injurious to the French Protestants, who could happily have dispensed with such compromising and, for them, useless friendship.

Public opinion in France accepted bluntly, then, the idea that "Protestants" were responsible for a regicide in cold blood, the worst possible kind. Or, if you like, that English regicides, monsters all, were all Protestants. The foundation of the Commonwealth was itself a sufficient testimony to the republican tendencies, at least in potential, of the Reformed tradition. Was a monarchy wise to harbor a people so little inclined to respect the prerogatives of its king? Were the innumerable and desperate declarations of loyalism made by the Huguenots and their emphatic adhesion to absolutism by divine right to be taken seriously? Were such professions, on the contrary, not to be deemed dubious in the light of the Protestants' inclination towards "republican" constitutions?

C. In fact, one only has to consult the *Discipline des Églises réformées de France*,[8] that charter of their internal organization, to perceive that the Presbyterian-synodal régime was one of assemblies, where decisions were made by a majority vote. To crown it all, a high number from the laity were in attendance, since each church sent two elders together with the minister to the provincial synods and elders also participated in national synods. Moreover, as a matter of principle, the *Discipline* explicitly rejected any notion of a hierarchy and established, in theory, a perfect egalitarianism among the ministers. On the ground, of course, and *de facto*, some pastors carried more weight in the synods, either by means of their eloquence, their knowledge or their personal authority. Claude, a minister at Charenton was nicknamed the "Emperor Claude" because his eloquence and prestige earned the support of his colleagues. Nonetheless, in theory, no pre-established hierarchy guaranteed him any more power than the most recently consecrated pastor. Was the conclusion not inevitable, then, that the monarchy was in complete harmony with the hierarchical pyramid of Catholicism, whilst a shocking disparity existed between the ecclesiastical

---

[8] The Discipline of the Reformed Churches of France, composed in the sixteenth century, established in detail their rules of organization.

organization of the Reformed Churches and that of the kingdom of France? James I had tellingly observed: "No bishop, no king."

These different considerations all led to the same conclusion: was it not a dangerous anomaly to welcome in an absolutist kingdom a religious minority with "republican" tendencies? There was a fundamental inconsistency between the state of mind desirable in the subjects of an absolutist monarch and the incipient "democracy" inseparable from affiliation to the Reformed Church. On the ground, Moïse Amyraut, the great theologian of Saumur, had rightly described the Reformed church in action as an aristocracy, since the elders were co-opted and came for the most part from among the leading citizens. But such arguments carried little weight. Thus, according to their enemies, the French Reformed Churches constituted within the kingdom of France a potential cancer that might flare up if stimulated by events capable of activating the tendency to subversion deemed inseparable from Protestantism. This was not to call the intentions of the Huguenots into question or to accuse them of hypocrisy in their proclamations of loyalism; it merely highlighted a latent danger. Article XXVI of the Confession of Faith of the French Reformed Churches affirmed the right to the public practice of religion, "even if opposed by Magistrates and Edicts"; article XL expressly outlined the duty of the Reformed Christian to be submissive to the duly appointed authorities, provided, however, "the Lord's empire stays intact." And the Huguenots were certainly acquainted with the verse in Acts (IV:19) which bids the believer to obey God rather than men.

It is possible, therefore, to draw up an anti-Protestant indictment exclusively based on political grounds, without taking into consideration the doctrinal errors which the Catholics attributed to the minority religion. Such political considerations certainly provided a significant ideological foundation, as it were a passive one, for the Revocation.

But the Edict of Fontainebleau and everything which preceded it—for the Revocation, let it be remembered, far from being an isolated incident, was instead the culmination of shifting political sands on a huge scale—took place when it did on the basis of favorable circumstances. If political considerations rendered the eradication of Protestantism in France *theoretically* desirable, the empirical evaluations triggered off the measures taken and the precise moment for the promulgation of the Edict of

Fontainebleau. As Émile Léonard has observed, the question it raises is why it had not happened much earlier![9]

The Revocation, as is well-known, depended on a multiplicity of factors. Let me mention in passing, first, the opportunity it gave the king to repair his reputation as the Most Christian King (*Roi Très Chrétien*), a reputation singularly tarnished by the remarkable absence of his troops in September 1683, at the raising of the siege of Vienna, under attack from the Turks. Second, the accession of James II to the throne of England in February 1685 and his quelling of the insurrection led by Monmouth was a godsend: England was now governed by a Catholic monarch. Third, given that since the Four Gallican Articles of the general assembly of the clergy in 1682 relations between the King of France and the Holy See had been very strained, the Sun King was aware of the political advantages to be reaped from forcing Pope Innocent XI to proffer his thanks and congratulations.[10]

Let us not lose sight, however, of the apparent summit of power reached by Louis XIV in those years—a power enabling him to annex Strasbourg during peacetime and apparently promising him complete freedom of action. Was it not attractive to think that he would be doing his kingdom and dynasty an immense service by delivering them once and for all from the Huguenot liability? Such was the state of affairs—it was thought, somewhat idiotically—that the Revocation would promote. For, if the Protestant people as a minority could easily be brought to heel by the Sun King in all his glory, future circumstances—such as a regency or the reign of a less absolutist monarch—might allow them to rear their heads once again.

But leaving aside these different motives, all of them well-known and all conspiring together to untie—in a radical way—the Gordian knot, I wish to consider for a moment two frequently more neglected observations able to shed light on the Revocation.

---

[9] Émile-G. Léonard, *Histoire générale du protestantisme*, 3 vols. (Paris, 1961). There is an English edition, 2 vols. (London, 1965-67).

[10] In fact, they were lukewarm and slow: see Jean Orcibal, *Louis XIV et les protestants* (Paris, 1951), 139-47.

a) First and foremost the theoretical positions that gave an appearance of utter legitimacy to court initiatives for the complete abolition of the *R.P.R.* I refer here to the development of a controversy that for several years had excelled in describing the Protestants not as the heretics they were and always will be but as schismatics, "separated brethren," an expression neither kindly nor innocent at the time. The Archbishop of Paris, Harlay de Champvallon, summed up the position in a brilliant phrase: "Cut down the schism and the heresy will dry out. . . ." Good-natured souls naively assume that the attribution of schism to the Huguenots reveals a departure from the harshness of controversy until that time. Let us rather believe the seventeenth-century eyewitnesses, who desperately insist on asserting their dogmas, or more exactly from the Catholic point of view, their heresies, for they were well aware that a tradition going back to Saint Augustine's treatment of the Donatists made the state or the prince responsible for the suppression of schism. Insofar as the Protestants saw themselves equated more and more with schismatics, they were aware of the increasing likelihood of civil measures being taken against them. In theory, persistence in heresy was punishable at the stake; meanwhile, schism called for therapeutic or pedagogic and radical disciplinary measures. That is to say, in a more popular idiom, schismatics were to be visited by a skillful combination of carrot and stick, to be administered by the secular arm. Consequently, one branch of anti-Protestant controversy tended to present the guided return of the Huguenots to mainstream Catholicism as a royal duty, as obviously the recommended methods of punishment and recompense could only be put into operation by the secular authorities. In theory, given that the Spanish Inquisition was highly disapproved of in France, these methods expressly excluded extreme solutions, such as capital punishment. Thus, capital punishment was only established for Huguenots in France on 1 July 1686 in order to try to stop the *désert* assemblies,[11] a decision pointing to the failure of the Edict of Fontainebleau. The identification of Huguenot with schismatic suggested instead the use of "gentle measures," "flower-strewn paths," in the phrase coined by Racine and used by the abbé Colbert. The measures, therefore, had to be constantly presented, albeit with a good deal of sophistry, not as aggressive sanctions but simply as a withdrawal of the king's "favors" from the minority or as favors

[11] "Desert wilderness"—a biblical allusion—was used to describe both the clandestine meetings and the clandestine reorganization of the French Reformed Churches. The meetings took place in open air, as far as possible from villages where the local authorities—in particular, the Catholic *curé* (the chief parish priest)—could be aware of the meeting.

graciously granted to submissive subjects, who recanted to please the king. From this angle, Louis XIV was in no way overreaching his prerogatives. He did not thereby become a despot but remained "the father of his people" when using his legislative powers to bring back the lost sheep to the bosom of the Roman Church. For he merely drew them by "favors" that he was entirely at liberty to refuse to bestow on those who persisted in heresy.

The strange amalgam of religion and politics proper to the *Ancien Régime* has its exact counterpart in England in the attitude to the Catholics, up until the reign of William III (1689-1702) and the foundation of an appreciable if still incomplete religious toleration. Such an amalgam allowed for the sanction of a patently religious attitude by construing it as an act of disobedience to the civil laws. Such was the justification for the bloody suppression of the attempt, inspired by Claude Brousson, to hold Protestant services in the open air in those areas of Languedoc and Dauphiné where they had been forbidden. The attempt was in principle and expressly non-violent and also in accordance with article XXVI of the Confession of Faith of the French Reformed Churches cited above. Nonetheless, in the eyes of the civil authorities, it constituted a patent infringement of the laws of the land and fell under the regulations for "illegal meetings." Punishment was meted out, then, if the authorities are to be believed, not for a religious conviction but for an act of disobedience to the prince. Such is the perpetual and fundamental clash: while some think to engage in a religious activity, demanded by their consciences, the powers that be punish—often ferociously—what they deemed a civil offense.

Now, this point of view provided the most enormous temptation, which the court did not resist, namely that of promulgating made-to-measure decrees, as it were, which in fact were traps for the Huguenots. With a Pharisaism which now seems naive, the Protestants as such in France (or the Roman Catholics in England) were not harassed, but only insofar as they infringed one of the laws of the land—a law conceived to spot them, like the Test Acts. Thus to sing a psalm or to pray in French could become a crime in the kingdom the Most Christian King.

The bewildering litany of decisions from the different *parlements* and the decrees, declarations and edicts concerning the *R.P.R,* which no-one has yet succeeded in classifying perfectly, too often evoke sometimes Kafka and at times "père Ubu."[12] Of course, these regulations were applied very unevenly: "the Christian easy-goingness," in Bayle's words,[13] or simply the common sense of many law-enforcing agents sufficed to make them null and void. Not to mention the legalistic sense of magistrates, very attached for example to the notion of paternal authority, who considered unacceptable the "conversion" to Catholicism of a seven-year old Huguenot child—even if a royal declaration had made it legal. Nevertheless, this orgy of regulations provided almost anyone with the means of accusing any or all French Protestants of infringing the law and all who availed themselves of them seem to have found therein the easy road to a good conscience.

b) Jean Orcibal[14] has demonstrated, and convincingly it seems, that there never was a "master-plan," carefully designed to break down the *R.P.R.* The court was groping, moving step by step, navigating by sight. The ultimate objective was clear but the way forward was roundabout and the Protestant question only came under close scrutiny after the Peace of Nijmegen (1678). After the *dragonnade*[15] in 1681, hopes were pinned on the *Avertissement pastoral*[16] of the clergy of France, a text knocked together *in extremis* at the end of the session, whose diffusion among all the consistories still in operation took many months without having the slightest effect.

Nonetheless the accumulation of decrees and declarations had created a sort of bottleneck. The so-called "new converts," thick on the ground after the *dragonnades*, were exempted for three years from payment of the *taille*[17] and enjoyed a moratorium on the capital of their debts. With the growth in their numbers, the economy of Languedoc was seriously disturbed and the court, to avoid undermining

---

[12] The hero of a book by Alfred Jarry, described in a grotesque and half surrealistic fashion as a ferocious tyrant.

[13] "Débonnaireté chrétienne."

[14] Cf. *supra* note 10.

[15] Soldiers—often dragoons—were forcibly lodged in Protestant households, which were obliged to feed them; those unwelcome and ruinous guests were incited to use every harassment to obtain from their hosts the recanting of their religious particularism.

[16] A "pastoral" letter of the bishops, who considered the Protestants in their respective dioceses as their lost sheep. As bishops and *intendants* jointly addressed themselves to the consistories, the negative answer was to be worded with great caution, not to appear as a subversive resistance to the civil authorities.

[17] The principal tax.

it further, had to abandon its project to abolish the sale of land at low prices by the Protestants who were beginning to leave France in great numbers. Moreover, the economy was not the only activity beset by anarchy as a result of the official decrees. Certain elementary requirements for the efficient administration of the kingdom had been jeopardized. In those areas where Protestant services had been forbidden and the minister banished—and they had become very numerous years before the Revocation—records were no longer made of the civil state of Protestants, whether baptism or death. A transitory *arrêt du conseil* of 15 September 1685, which appointed itinerant ministers paid by the *intendant* in each province and commissioned them to celebrate baptisms and marriages and to record deaths, bears witness to the concern felt in high places about a situation thoughtlessly created. It might be mentioned in passing that the same decree also reveals a complete ignorance of the *Discipline of the Reformed Churches*, which stipulates that baptism and marriages can only be celebrated during public worship. Moreover, at that particular time, a minister—without a church—could easily have aroused the quite justified suspicion of the Huguenots. But the court had begun to realize first, that the destruction of Protestant churches was not attracting the faithful to Mass; second, that since the cemeteries had been suppressed, the Huguenots were burying their dead on their lands and also along the roadside; third, that Huguenot children would long await a baptism considered peripheral to eternal salvation by their parents, even if baptismal registers were necessary to the records of the civil state. As for wedlock, it is not impossible that the first "common law marriages" were already beginning to appear during this period. Such unions were in evidence between well-matched young people, joined by notarial contract, blessed by their respective parents and whose joint existence, far from furtive, was so open and well-known that their Catholic neighbors considered them "married." For as long as the Huguenots had remained free to go to one of the few Protestant churches still standing in their region, they had been able to celebrate baptisms and marriages at the price of a long journey. But since the Declaration of 25 July 1685, this escape route had been closed.

It seems, then, that to a certain extent, the Revocation might also be considered as a measure destined to make a tangle of decrees and declarations—promulgated against the Huguenots over a period of twenty years—fall automatically into disuse. For the measures had succeeded in creating appreciable obstacles to the normal administration of the provinces where the Huguenots were numerous; by forcing the latter to the fringes of society, they had turned them into outlaws. In some respects, the Revocation appears as an attempt to annul provisions made to create difficulties for the Protestants but whose cumulative effect was a greater hindrance to the authorities themselves. The situation had come to the stage at which it would have been necessary either to go into reverse (to give the Protestants back their churches and ministers) or to go right on to the end. Now, it is well-known that Louis XIV believed that a prince should never reverse his decisions.

In conclusion: does the consideration of the anti-Protestant policies of Louis XIV as inspired in large measure by the politics of Reason of State—crudely bedecked in appropriate propaganda—undermine the role of the Gallican Church as an inspirational, indeed a decisive factor, as some have maintained? It seems not. For it merely shifts the weight of the fairly crushing responsibilities of the French Catholic clergy, without either diminishing or erasing them. Louis XIV observes in his *Mémoires*[18] that "a badly informed man cannot help thinking badly." Certainly the court was more than frivolous to ask the French Catholic clergy—the milieu most systematically hostile to the Edict of Nantes and French Protestants—for information about the latter. But once consulted, the prelates were most definitely not innocent in the highly deceptive picture they gave the king, almost passing over heresy to concentrate on schism; and even less so in the statement of affirmation that the passage from the Reformation to Rome could be easily made. This was a radical misjudgment, a wishful thinking or a calculated suppression of the religious and spiritual nature of the resistance to abjuration. To see therein only stubbornness and pride, if not a case of unadulterated bad faith, reveals a contemptuous sectarianism that does no honor to the priests who harbored it. On the one hand, in their desire to see the *R.P.R.* disappear from the kingdom, the Gallican clergy were acting in accordance with their vocation and for this they cannot be condemned. To do so would be to argue anachronistically. On the other, it appears that to their mind, too often at least, the end justified and, as it were, sanctified all the means—even the worst—which is grave indeed. The part taken by the clergy of some areas in that strange sacrilege, communion by coercion, is well-known. They could not have been unaware of the brutal methods used by the court and at least suspected—probably better than the

---

[18] Cf. Louis XIV, *Mémoires pour l'instruction du Dauphin*, ed. Charles Dreyss, 2 vols. (Paris, 1860), 2:95.

king himself—the nature of the *dragonnades*. Nonetheless, they delighted to dissem-
inate a soothing propaganda couched in unctuous language that, not content to
embellish the real state of affairs, also endeavored to mask and flagrantly deny it.
Here clerical ideology did not so much *inspire* policies as serve to *hide* them: the
Church of France hastened to raise a superb screen of seemliness destined to disguise
the state of affairs on the ground. Thus the Catholic clergy may have facilitated the
worst brutality by bringing all its religious and moral authority to the support of that
wretched and disparaging idea, namely that resistance to abjuration was inspired not
by scruples of conscience and personal integrity but by a stubborn intractableness,
feeding on an execrable pride, which the authorities were justified in crushing with the
utmost brutality.

Such a pitiably reductionist analysis of the existential problem faced by the
Huguenots undoubtedly explains how the apparent, immediate triumph of the anti-
Protestant policies of Versailles—the effort to crush a minority and force them to
conform—finally largely became a Pyrrhic victory. For, far from resolving problems
and calming conflicts, they multiplied and exacerbated them disastrously. As early
as July 1686, the shameless fiction of "gentle persuasion" was no longer tenable, given
that capital punishment awaited preachers and the galleys or life imprisonment both
those who tried to leave France, an emigration strictly forbidden to laymen (if
obligatory for the pastors) and those who attended *désert* Protestant services. These
open-air services in out-of-the-way places began at the start of a spring that also
witnessed the abstention of an overwhelming majority of new converts from the
fulfilment of their "Easter duties." And in August 1715, a few days before the death
of the Sun King, the first *désert* synod was about to be held, an organization which
was to undertake with success, the slow and clandestine reconstitution of the Reformed Churches of France.

The failure of the royal policies against the Protestants is to be explained by the
fact that the court did not possess the enormous means of coercion demanded by her
policies. Seventeenth-century France was neither a "totalitarian" régime in the
twentieth-century sense of the word, nor a police state. Persecution was never waged
either all the time, or everywhere simultaneously; the deeds were very far behind the
will.

The resistance of the Huguenots—both the new converts, who stayed in France without really recanting their faith, and that of the refugees who, in spite of terrible dangers, went to the "freedom countries"—was also obviously a decisive factor in the failure of the Revocation. Had it been guessed at, it could perhaps have changed the court's policies, or at least slowed them. So at this point comes the responsibility of the court's favorite informant in religious matters, that is, the Gallican high clergy. Motivated by triumphalist aspirations, they either knowingly or stupidly underestimated the Huguenot people's abhorrence of a real apostasy. This was an error of judgement born out of scornful hatred for the adversary, a hatred that was not only a political blunder, but first and foremost a moral fault.

The Revocation of the Edict of Nantes and Huguenot Migration to South Carolina

Jon Butler

Between 1675 and 1690, from 150,000 to 200,000 Huguenots fled their native France to escape Louis XIV's final attempt to extirpate Protestantism from his lands. These refugees initially settled in the nearest Protestant sanctuaries available to them, namely Geneva, Brandenburg-Hesse, the Netherlands, and England. But as prospects dimmed for returning to France, many sought new homes for a permanent exile. These second migrations took Huguenot refugees far from their native France and Europe to places as remote as South Africa, Russia, and South Carolina. In these new and permanent homes, the Huguenot refugees and their descendants experienced significant cultural and religious changes. Some of these alterations proved to be relatively innocuous. French weavers, chamey-dressers, and silversmiths became, for example, American (or British) farmers. But other changes proved more problematic. Huguenots who left France to preserve their religious tradition became Anglicans, Presbyterians, even Baptists. Men and women who had fled religious persecution profited from a slavery that victimized others. Is it possible that the commemoration of the Revocation of the Edict of Nantes will stimulate a scholarship that makes sense of these and other anomalies in the history of French Protestantism?

Understanding the Revocation and the Huguenot migration to South Carolina lifts up a remarkable coherence in the past, even amidst wrenching persecution and significant social and religious change. The Revocation was more than a catalyst for Huguenot flight from France. It predicted the very character of Huguenot migration to South Carolina. In turn, the Huguenot migration and fate of its participants reflected more than European exigencies or American opportunity. They bespoke processes of change and alteration that, after the Revocation, overtook French Protestantism everywhere. In short, the Revocation, diaspora, and assimilation were not discrete, isolated events. They were consecutive scenes in a major historical drama that historians long ago named "Le Refuge," but to which they are only now giving sustained attention.

On the surface, the Revocation appears to have been a remarkably simple event. On 17 October 1685, Louis XIV revoked the Edict of Nantes issued by Henry IV in 1598 to grant privileges of worship to Protestants. The result was an exodus from France of about 160,000 French men, women, and children. This would have been a massive exodus even in modern times. In fact, it was the largest population movement in early modern Europe aside from the expulsion of the Moors from Spain, and it was all the more remarkable in the face of crude transportation and a social milieu that limited population mobility for most people to relatively constricted regional movement.[1]

If the size of the Huguenot exodus suggests some complexities of the Revocation, its causes and results confirm them. No event is inevitable, of course, and Louis XIV could have achieved the same end—elimination of effective Protestant influence in France—by continuing the campaign of terror, beatings, and forced conversions to Catholicism that had begun in the late 1670s. Indeed, it is not at all clear that Louis and his advisors intended to revoke the 1598 Edict when they began intensive anti-Protestant pressure in the 1670s. Although the desire to eliminate Protestants and Protestant power was long standing, the Revocation itself was the child of the late 1670s' persecution, not its parent—an achievement Louis XIV had long desired but never dared hope was attainable until its very eve. The Revocation was, then, new as well as familiar—a single event occurring in October 1685 whose origins easily extended back into the previous decade.[2]

The exodus produced by the Revocation quickly demonstrated complexities that help explain many, if not all, the transformations that subsequently overtook refugees in South Carolina and elsewhere. The extraordinary demographic breadth of the exodus reveals the deep effect of government terrorism in Protestant France. Where young, single men had dominated voluntary migration even in the early modern era, the Huguenot diaspora sent large numbers of women, and often old women, out of France. Women headed as many as half the refugee households in late seventeenth-

---

[1] Samuel Mours, *Essai sommaire de géographie du protestantisme réformé français au XVIIe siècle* (Paris, 1966).

[2] Daniel Ligou, "La peau de chagrin (1598-1685)," in Robert Mandrou et al., *Histoire des Protestants en France* (Toulouse, 1977), 118-22. The expulsion of the Moors from Spain constituted early modern Europe's other major forced migration. For a general history of religious refugees see Frederick A. Norwood, *Strangers and Exiles: A History of Religious Refugees* (Nashville, 1969).

century London. Moreover, half of these women were over fifty-five years of age and some had reached their seventies, remarkably old by early modern standards. Children also comprised an unusually large proportion of the fleeing population. In refugee settlements at Cazand and Groede in the Netherlands, half the refugee households contained young children, and London's charity committees were frequently besieged with requests to help parents who had brought children—even infants—across the English Channel. In both instances, this Huguenot exodus paralleled the modern exodus of Vietnamese, Cambodians, and Laotians from southeast Asia to the United States.[3]

The exodus also sustained an extraordinary length and breadth. First, it stretched across a full decade. True, the peak of the refugee flight occurred in the year surrounding the Revocation Edict of October 1685. Robin Gwynn's careful accounting of refugee reception in London's French churches reveals that although a third of all London refugees of the 1680s arrived in two years between 1684 and 1686, two-thirds of them arrived in the five years preceding or following the 1685 Edict. Furthermore, the refugees came from a surprising variety of locales within France. If the south of France contributed the smallest percentage of London's refugees, in part this stemmed from the fact that its Protestants sustained the most persistent and violent resistance to Louis XIV's Revocation Edict. Still, every area witnessed some kind of exodus, so that geographical proximity of exile centers to the areas of Protestant strength determined the composition of the refugee population in the exile centers. Half of England's refugees (who formed the pool from which most Huguenot emigrants to South Carolina would be drawn) came from northern France; slightly less than a quarter each came from western and central France; and less than 5 percent came from southern France.[4]

These characteristics reveal how thoroughly the dramatic changes typical of refugee Huguenotism began in the Revocation and exodus, not in South Carolina or the

---

[3] Jon Butler, *The Huguenots in America: A Refugee People in New World Society* (Cambridge, Mass., 1983), 25, 29-30. Useful books describing recent refugees in America and their background include Keith St. Cartmail, *Exodus Indochina* (Auckland, 1983); Lesleyanne Hawthorne, ed., *Refugee: The Vietnamese Experience* (New York, 1982); and Nathan Glazer, ed., *Clamor at the Gates: The New American Immigration* (San Francisco, 1985).

[4] A. P. Hands and Irene Scouloudi, eds., *French Protestant Refugees Relieved through the Threadneedle Street Church, 1681-1687*, Huguenot Society of London, *Proceedings*, 49 (1971); Butler, *Huguenots in America*, 27-28.

other places of final exile settlement. For example, in the new refugee centers of London, Rotterdam, Amsterdam, and Geneva, French Protestantism was suddenly national where it previously had been local and regional, at least for most of the seventeenth century. The Huguenots' last national synod had met in 1659, and refugees in London and elsewhere had never before encountered so many different strains of French Protestant practice and tradition. In addition, the length of the exodus brought continuous upheaval and change to the exile communities for over a decade. It slowed community stability because the refugee population shifted so often between 1680 and 1690. Amidst the cycles of births and deaths that irrepressibly enlarged and depleted families, refugees also frequently moved from one place to another. Some ventured into the Dutch, German, or English countryside; others departed for even more distant places, such as Carolina or New York. The new anxieties and deepening impoverishment of *le refuge* now were beginning to impress themselves deeply upon the exiles. As in the Old Testament, an exodus initiated to preserve faith now was changing the people who had begun it.[5]

Changes already imbedded in the exodus from France quickly extended into the diaspora and directly touched the Huguenot emigration to South Carolina. With the help of demography we can now see what contemporaries may not have noticed: that the Huguenots who came to South Carolina (and probably Russia, South Africa, and other British colonies in North America) were not representative of the Huguenot population that fled France. This is most obviously demonstrated in emigrant ages. Extrapolations based on the well-known 1697 list of adult applicants for South Carolina subjectship reveal that two-thirds of the refugees' children were born in South Carolina; less than a fifth were born in France; and fewer than a twelfth were born in the European exile centers. The same pattern held true at the refugee community of New Rochelle in New York where a 1698 census allows us to document the refugees' actual ages, and probably also at the Narragansett settlement in Rhode Island. They point up major differences between Huguenot immigrants in America and refugees remaining in Europe. In short, the Huguenots who came to South Carolina composed a self-selected subgroup within the larger exodus population—something historians now call a "cohort"—distinguished chiefly by its relative youth. The exodus

5   Daniel Ligou and Philippe Joutard, "Les Déserts (1685-1800)," in Mandrou, *Histoire des Protestants en France*, 189-204.

from France sent many old Huguenots, especially women, out of the country. But the re-migration to new places of permanent exile involved younger unmarried or newly married Huguenots.[6]

Economic causes produced this change in emigrating populations. None of the European exile centers easily absorbed the refugees. This was true even of the Netherlands, the most tolerant and economically dynamic society in early modern Europe. It also proved true of England, where nagging popular anti-French prejudice and an erratic economy stimulated government promotion of Huguenot re-migration. But while many refugees were poor when they left France and others had been made poorer by their exodus, younger refugees most consistently developed strategies to change these conditions. They perceived all too correctly that the mounting success of Louis XIV's campaign against the Protestants precluded their return to France. And their exile experience scarcely induced them to remain in London and the other exile centers. For example, many South Carolina immigrants about whom we have specific evidence demonstrate direct experience with deep, seemingly hopeless, poverty. Daniel Huger and Pierre Gaillard came to South Carolina with servants and thereby received additional land from the proprietors. But most others—Jacques Varein, Charles Faucheraud, Pierre Poinsette, and Noé Royer, for example—had so consistently taken charitable aid for food, clothing, and lodging in London that their economic motive for South Carolina emigration is perfectly obvious.[7]

It is scarcely surprising then that complete strangers found it possible to lure young Huguenots into flight once again, this time to South Carolina. We do not know—and probably never will know—how the Carolina proprietors contacted René Petit and Jacob Guerard to bring some eighty French Protestants to the infant colony in 1679 to begin its first Huguenot emigration. But we do know that this first settlement *preceded* a promotion that, in turn, stimulated the emigration that brought most South Carolina Huguenots to the colony between 1682 and 1695. Only *after* the 1679 migration did the proprietors issue the promotion pamphlets directed at European

---

[6] "Liste de françois et suisses," The Huguenot Society of South Carolina, *Transactions*, 24 (1926): 27-46. The original manuscript of this list apparently is lost. The 1698 New Rochelle census is printed in *New York Genealogical and Biographical Record*, 59 (1928): 105-107. On other censuses and the youth of the American immigrants see Butler, *Huguenots in America*, 47-49, 57-58.

[7] Butler, *Huguenots in America*, chap. 2.

Huguenots, pamphlets that ultimately comprised a major portion of the colony's promotion literature. *Carolina, or a Description of the Present State of that Country* appeared in London in 1682 and *Nouvelle relation de Caroline* and *Plan pour former un établissement en Caroline* were published in French at The Hague in 1685 and 1686.[8]

Secular opportunities constituted the principal lures presented to the Huguenot refugees. The Carolina proprietors never ignored the religious issue, and promised the Huguenots safety and toleration. But these already were available in England, the Netherlands, Germany, and Switzerland. What was not readily available were livelihoods and economic security. Hence the paradox of Huguenot emigration: secular recruitment for religious refugees. The Carolina proprietors met this challenge quickly. Their promotion literature overran with fat descriptions of material opportunity. Equally telling, the one immigrant letter that survives from the 1680s—Louis Thibou's letter to Gabriel Bontefoy of 1686—replicates the proprietors' concern for economic opportunity. Thibou was ecstatic in recommending the colony to London refugees. Again, the reason was secular, not religious—"rivers very full of fish," "bountiful crops of peas, wheat, and garden-melons," Madeira grapes that were "sweet, winey and full of juice."[9]

Amidst these concerns for livelihood it is not surprising that traditional Huguenot religious institutions were not established until the late 1680s. If a minister accompanied the 1679 settlers or even those of 1682 and 1683, we either do not know so or must guess at his identity. Worse, the first Huguenot minister known to have preached there—Laurent Van den Bosch—might have encouraged the early immigrants to do without one. He arrived in 1684, was gone by 1685, and by his own account won little support there, probably because he very likely behaved as badly there as he did later in Boston, where he embarrassed Huguenots with his pro-Anglican sympathies, and in New Paltz, where he all too soon revealed himself as a wife-beating drunk. Still, the clerical void had been filled by the end of the decade.

---

[8] The best description of the Carolina promotion literature still is found in Hope Frances Kane, "Colonial Promotion and Promotion Literature of Carolina, 1660-1700," (unpublished Ph.D. dissertation, Brown University, 1930). Also see Gilbert Chinard, *Les réfugiés Huguenots en Amérique* (Paris, 1925), 62-63.

[9] Louis Thibou to [Gabriel Bontefoy], 20 September 1683, mss. coll., South Caroliniana Library, University of South Carolina, Columbia. See Appendix III.

Élie Prioleau arrived in about 1687, Pierre Robert followed in about 1692, and Laurent Trouillart arrived about 1693. By the mid-1690s, these three outnumbered the one Anglican and one Dissenting clergymen who served the colony's far larger English-speaking population.[10]

The refugees' concern for economic opportunity and their seeming inattention to religion did not escape contemporary notice. The first surviving criticism of Carolina as a Huguenot refuge concluded with a warning about religion. An anonymous French tract of 1686 turned tables on the proprietors and criticized Carolina as "the least agreeable colony in America." It was an undeveloped, ceaselessly waterlogged "charnelhouse" that produced bankruptcy and death. But its author, knowing the lure of naive claims, warned refugees who journeyed there and stayed nonetheless "not to leave their religion behind" but "retain it in such purity and sincerity, that they may render the place to which they may come, better than those whence they came, and be more assured of its permanent enjoyment."[11]

Through the next half-century, the processes of change introduced by the exodus and extended in the diaspora continued to structure the behavior of refugee Huguenots. Considering the importance of economic opportunity it is scarcely surprising to find wide-ranging occupational change common among the refugees. When Jacques Varein wrote to Gabriel Bontefoy in 1686 encouraging London refugees to settle in the infant colony, he did so because he saw their traditional skilled trades as particularly valuable to a predominantly agrarian society. He proved to be more than right. Old World skills were not irrelevant in this New World society. The evidence clearly indicates that emigrating Huguenots plied traditional skills in Carolina as merchants, silversmiths, blacksmiths, and silk producers. They even worked successfully as weavers and tailors, occupations that traditionally have been associated with urban societies but which proved remarkably useful in a new colony dependent on high-priced imported clothing.

---

[10] Lawrence Van den Bosch to Henry Compton, Bishop of London, 4 July 1685, in Worthington Chauncy Ford, "Ezéchiel Carré and the French Church in Boston," Massachusetts Historical Society, *Proceedings*, 52 (1919): 122-23; Arthur H. Hirsch, *The Huguenots of Colonial South Carolina* (Durham, N.C., 1928), 61; S. Charles Bolton, *Southern Anglicanism: The Church of England in Colonial South Carolina* (Westport, Conn., 1982), 19, 86; George Howe, *History of the Presbyterian Church in South Carolina* (Columbia, S. C., 1870), 100-116.

[11] "Remarks on the New Account of Carolina by a French Gentleman—1686," *The Magnolia*, n.s. 1 (1842): 226-30.

But the Old World skills also proved transitional. Although historians also often interpret occupational change as a denial of one's heritage and an indicator of something forced and unnatural, the evidence from South Carolina suggests that Huguenots pursued it willingly without coercion, without force, without rejecting their refugee tradition. The Huguenot men who applied for naturalization in 1697 described themselves in terms familiar to traditional French Protestant culture. They were, they wrote, weavers, chamey-dressers, throwsters, merchants, wheelwrights, saddlers, graziers, sailmakers, clockmakers, gardeners, doctors, watchmakers, goldsmiths, gunsmiths, blacksmiths, coopers, and shipwrights.[12]

Yet the South Carolina refugees also were pursuing another occupation: farming. While they used traditional trade and merchant terms to describe themselves in their 1697 naturalization petition, many of the same refugees also were obtaining land in utterly astonishing quantities. The South Carolina land records only describe property dispensed through direct government sale or distributed as inducements to importing servants and slaves; they ignore the burgeoning market of private sales. Still, the colony's land records alone reveal that by 1700 Huguenots had acquired at least 36,000 acres of land from the government—most of this necessarily given to first-generation refugees. In the next decade alone they and their descendants acquired yet another 68,000 acres from the government. By 1710, then, scarcely thirty years after their first arrival in the colony, Huguenot immigrants had acquired more than 104,000 acres through government sale and distribution.[13]

This astonishing Huguenot record makes the better known New England and Pennsylvania land acquisition patterns pale by comparison. Historians often explain settlement in both these more northerly areas by the lure of land. In fact, South Carolina easily outstripped its northern counterparts in its distribution of land to European immigrants. The English settlers who acquired land in seventeenth-century New England or in Pennsylvania before 1720 averaged less than an eighth of the 710 acres obtained by Huguenot immigrants in South Carolina. Even the largest New England and early Pennsylvania farmers usually acquired only 300 or so acres of

---

[12] "Liste de françois et suisses," The Huguenot Society of South Carolina, *Transactions.*

[13] Based on a survey of *Warrants for Land in South Carolina, 1672-1711*, ed. A. S. Salley, Jr., and R. Nicholas Olsberg (Columbia, S.C., 1973).

land, and their acquisitions came to less than half the *average* acreage acquired by first-generation Huguenot landholders in South Carolina.[14]

The South Carolina landholding record reflected paradoxical and important political and social realities in early South Carolina. In fact, widespread Huguenot landholding was remarkable because it flew in the face of a vigorous contemporary prejudice that produced political discrimination against Huguenots. The story is complex, but put in simplest terms, between 1695 and 1706 the Carolina assembly disenfranchised Huguenots. This happened for two reasons. Through their numerical dominance in Craven County Huguenot immigrants possessed considerable political power in a colony beset by many-sided political disputes among the English-speaking majority. Worse, some English colonists simply disliked the Huguenots however strong the immigrants' Protestantism or pathetic their exodus. In 1704, for example, the so-called "Dissenter" party demanded dissolution of the South Carolina assembly on grounds the franchise included "Jews, strangers, sailors, servants, negroes and almost every Frenchman in Berkeley and Craven Counties."[15]

Yet South Carolina's record in land distribution dramatically demonstrates the selectivity of early American nativist prejudice. In South Carolina it did not extend to economic policy, and its economic and even social constraints contrasted sharply with contemporary treatment of Africans or subsequent treatment of Catholics and Jews. Moreover, the South Carolina proprietors proved significantly more generous to Huguenots than Puritan and Quaker contemporaries were to Englishmen. New England and Pennsylvania authorities implemented relatively parsimonious land policies among both adherents and non-adherents, whether guided by fears of moral decay resulting from land gluttony or by a refusal to adopt a headright system that would encourage slaveholding, the source of much Huguenot land in South Carolina.

---

[14] On the New England patterns see Kenneth A. Lockridge, *A New England Town: The First Hundred Years* (New York, 1970), 71, and Charles S. Grant, *Democracy in the Connecticut Frontier Town of Kent* (New York, 1971), 13-16, 18-20, 56-62. For Pennsylvania patterns see James T. Lemon, *The Best Poor Man's Country: A Geographical Study of Early Southeastern Pennsylvania* (Baltimore, 1972), 42-70, and Mary Maples Dunn and Richard S. Dunn, eds., *The Papers of William Penn* (Philadelphia, 1981), 2:630-35.

[15] On the question of bigotry in South Carolina see Butler, *Huguenots in America*, 102-105. For an introduction to the problem of anti-immigrant prejudice in nineteenth- and twentieth-century America see two books by John Higham: *Strangers in the Land: Patterns of American Nativism, 1860-1925* (New Brunswick, N.J., 1965), and *Send These to Me: Immigrants in Urban America*, revised edition (Baltimore, 1984).

In addition, and somewhat surprisingly, Huguenot refugees themselves seem to have pursued landholding more aggressively than did their Puritan or Quaker contemporaries. Certainly, some refugees acquired very little land. Isaac Varry and Isaac Remich each received only 100 acres of land in 1694 and 1696 and obtained no more land from the government in the next decade. But others acquired enormous amounts of land. Powerful entrepreneurs like John Gaillard and Philippe Gendron obtained between 3700 and 4300 acres respectively and appear to have possessed sufficient capital to make much of it productive.

It was the breadth rather than the all too typical inequality of landholding that made the Huguenot record so remarkable in South Carolina. Virtually every Huguenot male known to be in Carolina in the 1690s received at least some land (fifty to one hundred acres) by 1710—a judgement made only on government land grant records. In contrast, New England Puritans often accepted increasingly restrictive land distribution policies well into the early eighteenth century. As the historian Philip Greven has demonstrated, men in Andover, Massachusetts, in their 50s and 60s obtained land only through inheritances from fathers who proved notoriously long-lived; they did not force town authorities to sell land to them or buy it elsewhere. Moreover, neither English, Welsh, Scottish, nor German immigrants in Pennsylvania ever matched the landholding record found among Huguenots in South Carolina, however appealing William Penn's promotional rhetoric.[16]

Widespread Huguenot ownership of land in South Carolina soon produced dramatic changes in the refugees' economic and cultural life. One of the less traumatic changes involved the disappearance of traditional Huguenot trades after 1700. The rich, complex occupational identifications that appeared on the 1697 naturalization petition soon gave way to a ubiquitous designation typical of all European settlers in the colony—"planter." By the 1720s, and even as early as the 1710s, Huguenot after Huguenot called no longer used the traditional French occupational classifications to identify himself. Little evidence suggests that they eschewed their old occupations deliberately. Although evidence on these matters is extremely thin, it does suggest that Huguenots used their old skills when it was desirable. Rather, the change was

---

[16] Land acquisition patterns are fully discussed in Butler, *Huguenots in America*, 96-97.

mental: now they thought of themselves as planters rather than weavers or chamey-dressers.[17]

"Merchant" and "silversmith" comprised the only significant remaining traditional occupations. Although the paucity of evidence about many things in the colony prevent us from appreciating the dimensions of the Huguenot merchant trades before 1710, continuing Huguenot involvement in the merchant business after 1710 is so obvious that their practitioners' names are an indelible part of the colony's pre-revolutionary history—Bedon, Boyer, Dart, Gendron, Huger, Légaré, and, of course, Manigault. The silversmith and goldsmith trade also remained a Huguenot enterprise. Huguenots comprised virtually the only silversmiths in the colony through the 1740s. Nicholas de Longemare, Jr., who worked in the 1710s, was among the most interesting, his account books revealing a renaissance man as busy with cattle pens and silk weaving as gold watches and engraving (unfortunately, virtually none of his work is known to survive). At the same time, a continuing Huguenot dominance in these trades reflected complexities in eighteenth-century British imperial trade patterns. New Huguenot silversmiths emigrated to Charleston from London where apprenticeship routines were heavily dominated by a Huguenot silversmith elite. In the main these new silversmiths often quietly displaced the older shopowners whose own children more often became merchants and planters.[18]

In turn, South Carolina's land distribution policies not surprisingly stimulated astonishing economic success among the Huguenot immigrants. Like the laws of physics, the assessment of wealth is relative, and it is not possible to document the wealth of a group without describing the society's economic structure, which, in South Carolina, is not possible until the 1730s. Still, the record of land acquisition suggests that first generation Huguenots were doing extremely well through the 1710s, and this seems confirmed by estate records of second-generation immigrants dying after 1730.

[17] The subject of occupational change in America has produced a large and often disputatious literature, nearly all of it on the nineteenth and twentieth centuries. For an introduction to the problem see Stephan Thernstrom, *The Other Bostonians: Poverty and Progress in the American Metropolis, 1880-1970* (Cambridge, Mass., 1973).

[18] Samuel G. Stoney, "Nicholas de Longemare, Huguenot Goldsmith and Silk Dealer in Colonial South Carolina," *South Carolina Historical and Genealogical Magazine*, 13 (1912): 38-69; E. Milby Burton, *South Carolina Silversmiths, 1690-1860* (Rutland, Vt., 1968); David R. McFadden, "Alexander Petrie and David Willaume, Jr.: Recent Acquisitions in Silver," *Bulletin*, Minneapolis Institute of Arts, 61 (1974): 35-39.

Judged by slaveholding—a good measure of economic success in a largely agrarian colony—second-generation Huguenots probably did better than English settlers. From the mid-1730s through at least 1745, 4.7 percent of English estates but 12.2 percent of Huguenot estates contained more than sixty-one slaves. In contrast, 54.8 percent of English estates but only 29.3 percent of Huguenot estates contained but 1-10 slaves.[19]

This general economic achievement never compensated for individual experiences. John You's pathetic estate of £13 in 1749 suggests that his own life was too akin to Suzanna Trezevant's, who took aid from Charleston's St. Philip's Parish in 1751 to relieve her sickness and to clothe her naked children. And the Huguenot economic boom levelled off by mid-century. After 1745, Huguenots lost their early advantage, and Huguenots and English settlers compiled estates that were distributed across the economic spectrum in every nearly equal proportions. Still, the Huguenots' general record of economic achievement at mid-century and earlier challenged the economic success of even English settlers in South Carolina. No other colonial immigrant group and few in the nineteenth and twentieth centuries matched them. By almost any standard, theirs was a remarkable achievement.[20]

South Carolina's land distribution policies propelled Huguenots toward a third major change as well—slaveholding. In one regard this was scarcely surprising. Slavery was common to all of Europe's New World societies. Huguenots in the French Antilles possessed slaves by the 1650s, and the surviving Protestant merchants of La Rochelle continued their deep involvement in the slave trade long after the Revocation. Yet, precisely because the South Carolina refugees were men and women of their own time as well as Huguenots, other models of behavior also were available to them. Huguenot clergymen in Europe had criticized slave trading and slave ownership. The Huguenot synod at Rouen condemned the slave trade in 1637, and refugee leaders in the Netherlands, including Pierre Jurieu, Rotterdam's famous millennialist émigré Huguenot minister, attacked slaveholding in the 1680s. In addi-

---

[19] Based on an analysis of Huguenot estates found in the Estate Inventories, 1736-65, South Carolina Archives, Columbia, S.C., as interpreted in light of colony-wide patterns described in Richard Waterhouse, "South Carolina's Colonial Elite: A Study in the Social Structure of a Southern Colony, 1670-1760," (unpublished Ph.D. dissertation, The Johns Hopkins University, 1973).

[20] Parish of St. Philip's, Charlestown, Vestry book, 1732-55, WPA transcript, South Caroliniana Library, 164.

tion, Carolina's Huguenot refugees were young men and women who had never before worked in a slaveholding economy. Finally, and most obviously, they were themselves victims of bigotry and coercion. Indeed, French Protestants at home and in exile would would continue to condemn the infamous example of Louis XIV's "galleys" on which imprisoned Huguenots toiled to serve Europe's Most Christian King until they were freed at the monarch's pleasure or died of exhaustion.[21]

Still, South Carolina Huguenots took to slaveholding early and enthusiastically. They were not alone, either as Huguenot refugees or as American colonists. English colonists were just beginning to purchase slaves in large numbers, and Huguenots quickly did likewise. Refugees in the New York settlement of New Rochelle, for example, bought slaves with such rapidity that as early as 1698 Africans comprised nearly 20 percent of the town's otherwise all-Huguenot population. Huguenots eclipsed this pattern in South Carolina. The catalyst was, again, the colony's land policy. It acted as both carrot and stick—carrot because it provided handsome rewards for importing slaves (fifty acres of land for each African imported), stick because it drove planters into a competition for agricultural production that simply could not be satisfied by any other means, such as the indentured servitude of Europeans (few Huguenots arrived as indentured servants even though conditions in London made them ideal prospects). Slaveholding thus became commonplace for virtually all Huguenot men in South Carolina. Once again, the land acquisition record between 1695 and 1710 suggests its early breadth, and estate records after 1730 confirm the pattern. From 1736 through the 1760s slaves could be found in 90 percent of all Huguenot estates.[22] Slaveholding capped the secular changes that typified Huguenot refugees in South Carolina and bespoke their ever widening departure from traditional French culture. Immigrants became landowners; skilled craftsmen became planters; planters became slaveholders. But, again, Old and New Worlds meshed as change occurred through transcendence, not rejection. Income provided through weaving, silk production, and wine growing bridged the processes of occupational change. Refugees shifted only slowly to the rice and indigo that would soon

---

[21] David Brion Davis, *The Problem of Slavery in Western Culture* (Ithaca and London, 1966), 109-110, 201. Also see Gabriel Debien, *Les esclaves aux Antilles françaises, XVIIe-XVIIIe siècles* (Guadeloupe, 1974), and Antoine Gisler, *L'esclavage aux Antilles françaises (17e-19e siècle)* (Fribourg, 1965).

[22] On early South Carolina economic development and slaveholding see Peter Wood, *Black Majority: Negroes in Colonial South Carolina from 1670 through the Stono Rebellion* (New York, 1974), 3-34.

typify all of South Carolina by the mid-eighteenth century. And occupational change affected human interrelationships through slavery. In fact, slavery became the fulcrum of both Huguenot success and change in South Carolina. Without slavery and the captive Africans who fueled it the Huguenots' extraordinary record of acquiring land—with all the implications of that land for refugee occupation and wealth—would have been impossible. Of course, Huguenots would have prospered in South Carolina; but they would not have prospered in the way that made their South Carolina experience so dramatic, so successful, and so significant.[23]

Huguenot slaveholding thereby emerged as the single most potent sign of Huguenot Americanization in secular life. Whatever the vicissitudes experienced by Huguenots themselves as hired servants, apprentices, or simple day laborers, they paled by comparison to the slave system Huguenots and Englishmen were building together in South Carolina. As slaveholding climbed from three or four slaves per owner in the 1690s to twenty and thirty in the 1710s, then escalated to 600 and 700 in the 1740s and 1750s among descendants of the Manigaults and Hugers, as Huguenots sat in the Carolina assemblies that wrote increasingly restrictive slave codes, and as Huguenot planters inserted notices in the South Carolina Gazette for runaway slaves or branded slaves with their initials—"BG" for Benjamin Godin, for example—they travelled a long, bitter road that would soon affect all Americans, not merely South Carolinians and Huguenots. That the Huguenot search for opportunity and safety took this path, and not some other, and that it proved so important to their assimilation, only made the Americanization of these refugees all the more ironic.[24]

Change—and Americanization—also occurred in religion where it centered on the decay of distinctive French Protestant religious traditions in the colony. This change also found its origins in the Revocation. The process began with the collapse of the Huguenot denominational structure at home. Nearly 80 percent of the Huguenot clergymen fled France (the remaining 20 percent conformed to Catholicism), stripping

---

[23] On the relationship between slavery and South Carolina economic development see ibid. and Converse D. Clowse, *Economic Beginnings in Colonial South Carolina, 1670-1730* (Columbia, S.C., 1971), 69-138.

[24] On slavery in South Carolina and elsewhere see Wood, *Black Majority*, and Edmund S. Morgan, *American Slavery, American Freedom: The Ordeal of Colonial Virginia* (New York, 1975). Morgan describes a similar paradox in the evolution of freedom and slavery in eighteenth-century Virginia.

Protestants of their traditional leadership. The inundation of the Huguenot exile centers with extraordinary numbers of refugee clergymen produced no Huguenot denomination in exile, however. The lay refugees could barely support themselves, and, in England, Anglican authorities demanded conformity to the Church of England before the ministers could receive financial aid, the only significant aid available to them in any form. As a result, the ministers pledged ecclesiastical loyalty to the Archbishop of Canterbury and never replicated the traditional denominational superstructure familiar to them in France. Therefore, they also proved unable to exercise collective supervision of Huguenot refugee congregations anywhere in the English-speaking world, including South Carolina.[25]

Few immediate problems occurred from the failure to form a Huguenot denomination in exile, at least in South Carolina. London's Threadneedle Street church acted as a clearinghouse for requests for clergymen, and the Charleston's French church turned to it successfully in 1699 and 1724 to obtain ministers. Fortunately also, the colony's French Protestant congregations acquired relatively long-lived ministers through the 1720s. Élie Prioleau served Charleston and, perhaps, several rural congregations for nearly fifteen years before he died in 1699; Laurent Trouillart apparently served both Charleston and the small Huguenot settlement in Berkeley County from the early 1690s until 1699, then Berkeley County alone until at least 1711; and Prioleau's Charleston successor, Paul L'Escot, served the Charleston congregation from 1700 until 1718.[26]

Yet the institutional failure evident in the Huguenot diaspora undermined the independent French congregations nonetheless. First, it produced as many pro-Anglican yearnings among South Carolina ministers as it had in England. Charleston's Paul L'Escot established a close relationship with Gideon Johnston, the Church of England commissary in Charleston. (Johnston's wife, Harriett, painted a pastel portrait of L'Escot's daughter that can be viewed at the Museum of Southern Decorative Arts in Winston-Salem, North Carolina.) In 1710, probably with Johnston's encouragement, L'Escot proposed to his French Church elders that he re-

---

[25] Robin D. Gwynn, ed., *A Calendar of the Letter Books of the French Church of London from the Civil War to the Restoration, 1643-1659*, Huguenot Society of London, *Publications*, 54 (1979): 2-26.

[26] Hirsch, *Huguenots in Colonial South Carolina*, 47-89.

ceive Anglican ordination, something already done by nearly all the ministers serving independent refugee churches in London and, probably, by three of South Carolina's Huguenot ministers (Laurent Trouillart, Philippe de Richebourg, and Pierre Robert), in addition to Francis Le Jau, a French-born, Anglican-ordained Huguenot who served the English-speaking Church of England parish of St. James Goose Creek.[27]

Second, the independent French churches missed the institutional resources that Huguenot denominational organization had provided in France. Early intra-congregational cooperation that is apparent in cooperative ministerial exchanges and rural support for a common Huguenot burying ground in Charleston appear to have slipped away by 1705. No institutional mechanisms existed to heal internal disputes in the congregations. Newly discovered letters of Charleston's Paul L'Escot in the Turrettini manuscripts at Geneva reveal that L'Escot feuded with his congregation for years about salary. After returning to England in 1719 he complained bitterly that the remarkably successful Huguenot laity forced him to live in a shabby fashion. He had built a small brick house and had acquired two slaves, but this was possible only after many years of saving. Indeed, he had been forced to sacrifice even these modest attainments when he returned to England. Salary disputes were common in all English denominations and among Huguenots in France as well. But where other religious groups possessed institutional mechanisms to intervene in solving them, Huguenot colloquies and synods now were non-existent.[28]

Third, the independent, institutionally isolated Huguenot congregations proved unable to resist the pressure of Anglican conformity. Part of the pressure involved straightforward support for church buildings and ministers' salaries. This may have been a special problem in areas like Berkeley County, which contained relatively small numbers of refugees, or even in Craven County, where the size of the so-called "Santee" settlement still may have been too small to support a minister well despite Huguenot economic success. Part of the pressure involved ministerial and lay support for latitudinarian Anglican theology, an unsurprising development rooted in the rise

---

[27] Butler, *Huguenots in America*, 38, 112-13.

[28] Paul L'Escot to Jean Alphonse Turrettini, May 25, 1719, Turrettini mss. (ms. fr. 488), Bibliothèque publique et universitaire, Geneva. See also Eugène G. T. De Bude, ed., *Lettres inédites adressées de 1686 à 1737 à J. A. Turrettini* (Paris and Geneva, 1887), 2:201-31; Gideon Johnston, "The Present State of the Clergy in South Carolina," [1713], in Hirsch, *Huguenots in Colonial South Carolina*, 297-309.

of doctrinal heterogeneity, including Arminianism, among seventeenth-century French Protestants.[29]

But part of the pressure also was coercive. That is, it involved the pressure of law and government activity that encouraged Huguenot men and women to do something that, without it, they might not otherwise have done. This coercion developed between 1700 and 1710 as the by-product of a complex dispute about establishing the Church of England in South Carolina. Although we never will know precisely what direct and indirect roles Huguenots played in the dispute, its effect on them is relatively clear. No rural South Carolina Huguenot congregation—meaning two surviving congregations, one at Santee, the other in Berkeley County—agreed to Anglican conformity except in the context of Anglican establishment. Government support for their ministers was not forthcoming without that establishment, and this occurred with passage of the 1706 Church Act that established the Church of England as the colony's government-sanctioned ecclesiastical establishment.[30]

Consequently, the earliest religious "Americanization" of South Carolina's Huguenots took a form that would have been unlikely had it occurred even twenty years later: it was largely Anglican rather than Dissenting. In contrast to Boston refugees who joined Congregational churches, New York refugees who distributed themselves amongst a wide variety of congregations, or even French-speaking Swiss colonists who arrived in South Carolina in the 1750s and 1760s and who often became Presbyterians or Baptists, first- and second-generation South Carolina Huguenots turned to the Church of England when they altered their denominational identity. If this Anglican Americanization seems somehow "un-American," it is helpful to remember that it reflected America as it was before 1720, not the America that would emerge even by 1760.[31]

---

[29] Mandrou, *Histoire des Protestants en France*, 134-41.

[30] The 1706 South Carolina Church Act and the Huguenot role in passing it has been the subject of much vexed discussion, some of it badly informed. The most dependable accounts are found in Clarence Ver Steeg, *Origins of a Southern Mosaic* (Athens, Ga., 1975), 30-53, and Amy Ellen Friedlander, "Carolina Huguenots: A Study in Cultural Pluralism in the Low Country, 1679-1768," (unpublished Ph.D. dissertation, Emory University, 1979), 147-55.

[31] Butler, *Huguenots in America*, 84-85, 169-73, 194-96; Jay Dolan, *The Immigrant Church: New York's Irish and German Catholics* (Baltimore, 1975); Higham, *Send These to Me*, 21-22.

Finally, Huguenot resistance to religious Americanization also was shaped by the exodus and diaspora. The failure to re-establish the traditional Huguenot ecclesiastical institutions and the pro-Anglican sympathies of most if not all Huguenot clergymen placed resistance in lay hands. But the deep economic and social changes then occurring among these lay men and women made them all the more sensitive to apparent reversals of their Huguenot tradition. Moreover, they were knowledgeable about London's so-called "French Prophets," refugees from the Camisard Wars of the late 1690s who condemned the Anglican conformity of London's Huguenot ministers there and emphasized radical piety, millenarianism, and miraculous healing.[32]

The result was a lay-led resistance in South Carolina that itself became ever more radical and untraditional. Sometime around 1712 refugees in Berkeley County led by Nicholas or Abel Bochet and occasionally but erratically reinforced by the clergyman John La Pierre bitterly condemned Anglican innovations introduced after 1706. This protest waned but was followed by one far more dangerous. Termed the "Dutartre Affair," it actually involved members of at least four refugee families—Boineau, Dutartre, Lesad, and Rembert. It also took the dissident Huguenots far from tradition as they imbibed sabbatarianism, millennialism, a short-lived pacificism, and, most notoriously, homicide, in the death of an English magistrate married to a Huguenot woman.[33]

The subsequent execution of three dissident leaders silenced resistance to Anglican conformity and smoothed the path for complete Huguenot assimilation into the colony's emerging religious structure. Charleston's French Church, the only independent Huguenot congregation in the colony, increasingly took its support from Huguenot descendants who had become active members of other denominations. Then, as the colony's denominational spectrum broadened after 1740, these descendants moved beyond Anglicanism to become Presbyterians, Baptists, and, much later,

---

[32] Hillel Schwartz, *The French Prophets: The History of a Millennarian Group in Eighteenth-Century England* (Berkeley and Los Angeles, 1980).

[33] The most recent discussion of the Dutartre affair properly places it in its broader intellectual and religious context: David Lovejoy, *Religious Enthusiasm in the New World: From Heresy to Revolution* (Cambridge, Mass., 1985), 172-75. Also see Butler, *Huguenots in America*, 119-20, and the single contemporary description on which all secondary accounts are based: Alexander Garden, *Take Heed How Ye Hear* (Charleston, 1741), 29-38.

Methodists. Still, some acknowledged their heritage at their deaths. As happened at funerals conducted by the minister at St. Philip's and recorded in that church's records, they would have their corpse carried down the street to the French Church, there to be interred in the "French Yard."[34]

What, then, had happened to South Carolina's Huguenots? They had arrived in the 1670s, 1680s, and 1690s seeking opportunity and safety following revocation of their privileges of worship in France and a dismal exile in Europe. Once in South Carolina, they had undergone major changes. Artisans and craftsmen had become planters. Religious refugees had become slaveholders. Protestants had remained neither French nor Huguenot, first becoming Anglicans, then Presbyterians, Baptists, and Methodists. In all, they had become Americans—British Americans to be sure, but Americans nonetheless, for they had undergone Americanization long before there was a United States.

As these changes occurred, had Huguenots betrayed their past, their tradition, their heritage? The answer returns us to the point at which we began—the Revocation. French Protestantism changed everywhere in its aftermath, not merely in South Carolina or, for that matter, Germany, Denmark, Russia, South Africa, everywhere the diaspora took it. In all these places it slowly disappeared. After 1720 it would rarely serve as a cohesive center for an aggressive, articulate refugee culture anywhere. Everywhere Huguenots assimilated and changed.

But change did not occur merely among exiles. It occurred at home too by creating a French Protestantism remarkably different from pre-Revocation Huguenotism, just as the rise of a planter class, slaveholding, and Anglican conformity transformed Huguenot refugees in South Carolina. The Camisard Wars in southern France and the period of the so-called "Church of the Desert" that extended into the 1720s deeply altered French Protestantism. The movement became radicalized, at least temporarily. Visions, apparitions, miraculous healings, and female leadership so often typified these years that they have long provided commentators and historians with vivid materials about "enthusiastic" religion—vivid if one likes such enthusiasm, scandalous if one does not. French Protestantism also became

---

[34] For miscellaneous references to these funeral practices see A. S. Salley, ed., *Register of St. Philip's Parish, 1720-1758* (Columbia, S. C., 1971).

overwhelmingly bourgeois. It lost its aristocratic support in the early seventeenth century; now, after the Revocation, it lost artisan, laborer, and peasant support. No one who remembered the movement of the 1660s could have been anything but astonished by the strangely homogeneous and small congregations.[35]

So we come back to the Revocation. If we wonder why we commemorate this event, the answer lies in its effects. It did not merely send Protestants out of France, though it certainly did that. The Revocation reshaped French Protestantism. It prevented French Protestants from sustaining their past, and it rewrote their future. In the process it touched every individual who imbibed Protestantism in France. Whether they remained at home or whether they fled, they and their immediate descendants certainly changed as much in a single lifetime as those of us born into modern society would care to do. This is why we commemorate the Revocation of the Edict of Nantes. It enveloped everything it touched, whether in France, in the European exile centers, or even in the solitude of the South Carolina low country.

---

[35] Ligou and Joutard, "Les Déserts (1685-1800)," in Mandrou, *Histoire des Protestants en France*, 189-215. On political as well as religious thought elsewhere in the diaspora see two works by Elisabeth Labrousse: *Bayle*, trans. Denys Potts (New York, 1983), and "The Political Ideas of the Huguenot Diaspora (Bayle and Jurieu)," in *Church, State and Society under the Bourbon Kings of France*, ed. Richard M. Golden (Lawrence, Kan., 1982), 222-83.

Chronological Table

1555 Peace of Augsburg (25 September)

1562 Beginning of French Wars of Religion (April)

1572 St. Bartholomew's Day Massacre (23-24 August)

1589 Henry IV becomes king (2 August)

1593 Abjuration of Henry IV (25 July)

1598 Edict of Nantes (13 April)
      Peace of Vervins with Spain (2 May)

1610 Assassination of Henry IV (14 May)
      Louis XIII becomes king

1618-48 Thirty Year's War (23 May 1618—24 October 1648)

1620 Government conquest of Béarn (October)

1621-22 Wars between the government and the Huguenots (April-November
      1621 and March-October 1622)

1622 Peace of Montpellier (19 October)

1624 Cardinal Richelieu enters the king's council (29 April);
      becomes principal minister (13 August)

1625-26 Wars between the government and the Huguenots
      (January 1625—6 February 1626)

1626 Peace of La Rochelle (5 February)

1627-29 Wars between the government and the Huguenots

1627-28 Siege of La Rochelle (10 August 1627—28 October1628)

1629 Grace of Alais (Alès) (28 June)

1637 Slave trade condemned by Huguenot synod at Rouen

1642 Death of Cardinal Richelieu (4 December)

1642-60 Puritan Revolution in England

1643 Death of Louis XIII (14 May)
      Louis XIV becomes king

1648 Peace of Westphalia (24 October)

1648-53 Revolts of the parlementary and noble *Frondes*
        (August 1648—July 1653)

1649 Regicide of Charles I of England (30 January)

1652 Royal Declaration of Saint-Germain (21 May)

1659 Peace of the Pyrenees with Spain (7 November)
      Last Huguenot national synod, at Loudun (November)

1660 Restoration of Charles II in England (29 May)

1661 Beginning of personal rule of Louis XIV (9 March)

1667-68 War of Devolution (24 May 1667—2 May 1668)

1672-78 Dutch War (7 April 1672—10 August 1678)

1676 Creation of the Bureau of Conversions (November)

1680 *Richmond* arrives with Huguenots in South Carolina (30 April)

1681 Annexation of Strasbourg (30 September)
      Dragonnades in Poitou

1682 Four Gallican Articles of the general assembly of the clergy (22 March)

1683 Battle of Kahlenberg ends siege of Vienna by the Ottoman Turks
      (12 September)

1684 Truce of Ratisbon (15 August)

1685 James II becomes king of England (6 February)
      Revocation of the Edict of Nantes (17 October)

1688 Glorious Revolution in England (December)

Appendix I

The Edict of Nantes*

HENRY, by the Grace of God, King of *France,* and *Navarre*, to all Present, and to Come, greetings. Among the infinite Mercies that God hath pleased to bestow upon us, that most Signal and Remarkable is, his having given us Power and Strength not to yield to the dreadful troubles, Confusions, and Disorders, which were found at our coming to this Kingdom, divided into so many Parties and Factions, that the most Legitimate was almost the least, enabling us with Constancy in such manner to oppose the Storm, as in the end to surmount it, reducing this Estate to Peace and Rest; For which, to Him alone be given the Honour and Glory, and us the Grace to acknowledge our obligation, in having our Labours made use of for the accomplishing so good a work, in which it hath been visible to all, that we have not only done what was our Duty, and in our Power, but something more than at another time, would (peradventure) have been agreeable to the Dignity we now hold; as in not having more Care, than to have many times so freely exposed our own Life. And in this great concurrence of weighty and perillous Affairs, not being able to compose all at one and the same time, We have chosen in this order; First to undertake those who were not to be suppressed but by force, and rather to remit and suspend others for some time, who might be dealt with by reason, and Justice: For the general difference among our good Subjects, and the particular evils of the soundest parts of the State, we judged might be easily cured after the Principal cause (the continuation of the Civil Wars) was taken away, in which we have, by the blessing of God, well and happily succeded, all Hostility and Wars through the Kingdom being now ceased, and we hope he will also prosper us in our other affairs, which remain to be composed, and that by this means we shall arrive at the establishment of a good Peace, with tranquility and rest, (which hath ever been the end of all our vows and intentions) as all the reward we desire or expect for so much pains and trouble, as we have taken in the whole course of our Life. Amongst our said affairs (towards which it behooves us to have patience) one of the principle hath been, the many complaints we received from divers of our Provinces and Catholick Cities, for that the exercise of the

---

* From Edmund Everard. *The Great Presures and Grievances of the Protestants in France* (London, 1681). Except for several egregious mistakes, Everard's translation has not been altered.

Catholick Religion was not universally re-established, as is provided by Edicts or Statutes heretofore made for the Pacification of the Troubles arising from Religion; as also the Supplications and Remonstrances which have been made to us by our Subjects of the reformed Religion, as well upon the execution of what hath been granted by the said former Laws, as that they desire to have some addition for the exercise of their Religion, the liberty of their Consciences and the security of their Persons and Fortunes; presuming to have just reasons for desiring some inlargement of Articles, as not being without great apprehensions, because their Ruine hath been the principal pretext and original foundation of the late Wars, Troubles, and Commotions. Now not to burden us with too much business at once, as also that the fury of War was not compatible with the establishment of Laws, how good soever they might be, we have hitherto deferred from time to time giving remedy herein. But now that it hath pleased God to give us a beginning of enjoying some Rest, we think we cannot imploy our self better, than to apply to that which may tend to the glory and service of his holy name, and to provide that he may be adored and prayed unto by all our Subjects: and if it hath not yet pleased him to permit it to be in one and the same form of Religion, that it may at the least be with one and the same intention, and with such rules that may prevent amongst them all troubles and tumults: and that we and this Kingdom may always conserve the glorious title of most Christian, which hath been by so much merit so long since acquired, and by the same means take away the cause of mischief and trouble, which may happen from the Actions of Religion, which of all others are most prevalent and penetrating. For this cause, acknowledging this affair to be of the greatest importance, and worthy of the best consideration, after having considered the papers of complaints of our Catholick subjects, and having also permitted to our Subjects of the Reformed Religion to assemble themselves by Deputies, for framing their complaints, and making a collection of all their Remonstrances; and having thereupon conferred divers times with them, viewing the precedent Laws, we have upon the whole judged it necessary to give to all our said Subjects one general Law, Clear, Pure, and Absolute, by which they shall be regulated in all differences which have heretofore risen among them, or may hereafter rise, wherewith the one and other may be contented, being framed according as the time requires: and having had no other regard in this deliberation than solely the Zeal we have to the service of God, praying that he would henceforward render to all our subjects a durable and Established peace. Upon which we implore and expect

88

from his divine bounty the same protection and favour, as he hath alwayes visibly bestowed upon this Kingdom from our Birth, during the many years we have attained unto, and give our said Subjects the grace to understand, that in observation of this our Ordinance consisteth (after that which is their duty toward God and us) the principal foundation of their Union, Concord, Tranquility, Rest, and the Re-establishment of all this Estate in its first splendor, opulency and strength. As on our part we promise to cause all to be exactly observed, without suffering any contra-diction. And for these causes, having with the advice of the Princes of our Blood, other Princes and Officers of our Crown, and other great and eminent Persons of our Council of State, being near us, well and diligently weighed and considered all this affair; We have by this Edict or Statute perpetual and irrevocable said, declared, and ordained, saying, declaring, and ordaining;

1. That the memory of all things passed on the one part and the other, since the beginning of the month of *March*, 1585 untill our coming to the Crown, and also during the other precedent troubles, and the occasion of the same, shall remain ex-tinguished and suppressed, as things that had never been. And it shall not be Lawfull or permitted to our Attorneys General, nor other person or persons whatsoever, publick or private, in any time, or for any occasion whatsoever it may be, to make mention thereof, Process or Prosecution in any Courts or Jurisdiction whatsoever.

2. We prohibit to all our subjects of what State and Condition soever they be, to renew the memory thereof, to attaque, resent, injure, or provoke one the other by reproaches for what is past, under any pretext or cause whatsoever, by disputing, contesting, quarrelling, reviling, or offending by factious words; but to contain them-selves, and live peaceably together as Brethren, Friends, and fellow-Citizens, upon penalty for acting to the contrary, to be punished for breakers of Peace, and disturbers of the publick quiet..

3. We ordain, that the Catholick Religion shall be restored and re-established in all places, and quarters of this Kingdom and Countrey under our obedience, and where the exercise of the same hath been intermitted, to be there again, peaceably and freely exercised without any trouble or impediment. Most expresly prohibiting all persons of what State, Quality, or Condition soever, upon the penalties before-mentioned not to trouble, molest, or disquiet the Ecclesiasticks in the celebration of

Divine Service, injoyning of receiving of Tythes, the fruits and Revenues of their Benefices, and all other Rights and Duties belonging to them: and we command, that all those who during the troubles, have invaded Churches, Houses, Goods, and Revenues belonging to the Ecclesiasticks, and those who detain and possess them, to deliver over to them the intire possession thereof with a peaceable enjoyment. and with such rights, liberties, and security as they had before they were deseized. Most expresly forbidding to those of the Reformed Religion, to Preach or exercise their said Religion in the Churches, Houses, and habitations of the said Ecclesiasticks.

4. It shall be the choice of the said Ecclesiasticks to buy the Houses and Structures built upon their ground in profane places, and made use of against their wills during the troubles, or compell the possessors of the said buildings to buy the ground according to the estimation that shall be made by skilfull persons, agreed upon by both Parties: And to come the better to an agreement, the Judges of the place shall provide such for them, except the said Possessors will try the Title to whom the places in question belong. And where the said Ecclesiasticks shall compell the possessors to buy the ground, the purchase-money if of estimation, shall not be put in their hands, but shall remain charged in the possessors hands, to make profit thereof at five *per Cent,* untill it shall be imployed to the profit of the Church, which shall be done within a Year. And after that time, if the Purchaser will not continue any longer at the said interest, he shall be discharged thereof by consigning the money to a responsible person, with the authority of the Justice. And for such places as are Sacred, advice shall be given therein by the Commissioners who shall be ordained for the execution of the present Edict, for which we shall provide.

5. Nevertheless the ground and foundation of places used for the reparation and fortification of Cities and places in our Kingdom, and the materials imployed therein, may not be sold nor taken away by the Ecclesiasticks, or other persons publick or private, untill the said reparations and fortifications shall by our order be demolished.

6. And not to leave any occasion of trouble and difference among our Subjects, we have permitted and do permit to those of the Reformed Religion, to live and dwell in all the Cities and places of this our Kingdom and Countreys under our obedience, without being inquired after, vexed, molested, or compelled to do any thing in Religion, contrary to their Conscience, nor by reason of the same be searched after in

houses or places where they live, they comporting themselves in other things as is contained in this our present Edict or Statute.

7. We also permit to all Lords, Gentlemen and other Persons, as well inhabitants as others, making profession of the Reformed Religion, having in our Kingdom and Countreys under our obedience, high Justice as chief Lord (as in *Normandy*) be it in property or usage, in whole, moiety, or third part, to have in such of their houses of the said high Justice or Fiefs, as abovesaid (which they shall be obliged to Nominate for their principall residence to our Bayliffs and chief Justice each in their jurisdiction) the exercise of the said Religion as long as they are Resident there, and in their absence, their wives or families, or part of the same. And though the right of Justice or whole Fief be controverted; nevertheless the exercise of the said Religion shall be allowed there, provided that the abovesaid be in actual possession of the said high Justice, though our Attorney General be a Party. We permitting them also to have the said exercise in their other houses of high Justice or Fiefs abovesaid, so long as they shall be present, and not otherwise: and all, as well for them, their families and subjects, as others that shall go thither.

8. In the Houses that are Fiefs, where those of the said Religion have not high Justice, there the said Exercise of the Reformed Religion shall not be permitted, save only to their own Families, yet nevertheless, if other persons, to the number of thirty, besides their Families, shall be there upon the occasion of Christenings, Visits of their Friends, or otherwise, our meaning is, that in such case they shall not be molested: provided also, that the said Houses be not within Cities, Burroughs, or Villages belonging to any Catholick Lord (save to us) having high Justice, in which the said Catholick Lords have their Houses. For in such cases, those of the said Religion shall not hold the said Exercise in the said Cities, Burroughs, or Villages, except by permission of the said Lords high Justices.

9. We permit also to those of the said Religion to hold, and continue the Exercise of the same in all the Cities and Places under our obedience, where it hath by them been Established and made publick by many and divers times, in the Year 1586, and in 1597, until the end of the Month of *August*, notwithstanding all Decrees and Judgements whatsoever to the contrary.

10. In like manner the said Exercise may be Established, and re-established in all the Cities and Places where it hath been established, or ought to be by the Statute of Pacification, made in the Year 1577, the particular Articles and Conferences of *Nerat*[1] and *Fleux*,[2] without hindering the Establishment in places of Domain, granted by the said Statutes, Articles, and Conferences for the Places of Baliwicks, or which shall be hereafter, though they have been alienated to Catholicks, or shall be in the future. Not understanding nevertheless that the said Exercise may be re-established in the Places of the said Domain, which have been heretofore possessed by those of the said Reformed Religion, which hath been in consideration of their persons, or because of the privilege of Fiefs, if the said Fiefs are found at present possessed by persons of the said Catholick Religion.

11. Furthermore, in each ancient Bailiwick, Jurisdiction and Government, holding place of a Bailiwick with an immediate Appeal (without mediation) to the Parliament,[3] We ordain, that in the Suburbs of a City, besides that which hath been agreed to them by the said Statute, particular Articles and Conferences; and where it is not a City, in a Burough or Village, the Exercise of the said Reformed Religion may be publickly held for all such as will come, though the said Bailiwicks, chief Jurisdictions and Governments have many places where the said Exercise is established, except, and be excepted the Bailiwick, new created by the present Edict or Law, the Cities in which are Arch-Bishops and Bishops, where nevertheless those of the said Reformed Religion are not for that reason deprived of having power to demand and nominate for the said Exercise certain Burroughs and Villages near the said Cities: except also the Signories belonging to the Eccliasisticks, in which we do not understand, that the second place of Bailiwicks may be established, those being excepted and reserved. We understanding under the name of ancient Bailiwicks, such as were in the time of the deceased King *Henry*, our most Honoured Lord and Father in Law, held for Bailiwicks, chief Justice-ships and Governments, appealing without intercession to our said Courts.

---

[1] Nérac.

[2] Fleix.

[3] The French *parlement*, a sovereign judicial institution.

12. We don't understand by this present Statute, to derogate from the Laws and Agreements heretofore made for the Reduction of any Prince, Lord, Gentleman, or Catholick City under our Obedience, in that which concerns the exercise of the said Religion, the which Laws and Records shall be kept and observed upon that account, according as shall be contained in the Instructions given the Commissioners for the execution of the present Edict or Law.

13. We prohibit most expresly to all those of the said Religion, to hold any Exericise of the same as well by Ministers preaching, discipling of Pupils, or publick instruction of Children, as otherways, in this our Kingdom or Countries under our Obedience, in that which concerns Religion, except in the places permitted and granted by the present Edict or Law.

14. As also not to exercise the said Religion in our Court, nor in our Territories and Countries beyond the Mountains, nor in our City of *Paris,* nor within five Leagues of the said City: nevertheless those of the said Religion dwelling in the said Lands and Countries beyond the Mountains, and in our said City, and within five Leagues about the same, shall not be searched after in their Houses, nor constrained to do any thing in Religion against their Consciences, comporting themselves in all other things according as is contained in our present Edict or Law.

15. Nor also shall hold publick Exercise of the said religion in the Armies, except in the Quarters of the principal Commanders, who make profession of the same, except nevertheless where the Quarters of our person shall be.

16. Following the second Article of the Conference of *Nerat*, we grant to those of the said Religion power to build Places for the Exercise of the same, in Cities and Places where it is granted them, and that those shall be rendered to them which they have heretofore built, or the Foundations of the same in the condition as they are at present, even in places where the said Exercise was not permitted to them, except they are converted into another nature of Building: In which case there shall be given to them by the Possessors of the said Buildings, other Houses and Places of the same value that they were before they were built, or the just elimination of the same, according to the Judgement of experienced persons, saving to the said Proprietors and Possessors, their Tryal at Law to whom they shall belong.

17. We prohibit all Preachers, Readers, and others who speak in publick, to use any words, discourse, or propositions tending to excite the People to Sedition; and we injoin them to contain and comport themselves modestly, and to say nothing which shall not be for the instruction and edification of the Auditors, and maintaining the peace and tranquillity established by us in our said Kingdom upon the penalties mentioned in the precedent Statutes. Expressly injoyning our Attorney Generals, and their Substitutes, to inform against them that are contrary hereunto, upon the penalty of answering therefore, and the loss of their Office.

18. Forbidding also to our Subjects, of what Quality and Condition soever they be, to take away by force or inducement, against the will of their Parents, the Children of the said Religion, to Baptize or Confirm them in the Catholick Church; as also we forbid the same to those of the said Reformed Religion upon pain of being exemplarily punished.

19. Those of the Reformed Religion shall not be at all constrained, nor remain obliged by reason of Abjurations, Promises, and Oaths, which they have heretofore made, or by caution given concerning the practice of the said Religion, nor shall therefore be molested or prosecuted in any sort whatsoever.

20. They shall also be obliged to keep and observe the Festivals of the Catholick Church, and shall not on the same days work, sell, or keep open shop, nor likewise the Artisans shall not work out of their shops, in their chambers or houses privately on the said Festivals, and other dayes forbidden, of any trade, the noise whereof may be heard without by those that pass by, or by the Neighbours: the searching after which shall notwithstanding be made by none but the Officers of Justice.

21. Books concerning the said Reformed Religion shall not be printed or sold publickly, save in the Cities and places where the publick exercise of the said Religion is permitted. And for other Books which shall be printed in other Cities, they shall be viewed and visited by our Theological Officers, as is directed by our ordinances. Forbidding most expresly the printing, publishing, and selling of all Books, Libells, and writings defamatory, upon the penalties contained in our Ordinances, injoyning all our Judges and Officers to seize the same.

94

22. We ordain, that there shall not be made any difference or distinction upon the account of the said Religion, in receiving Scholars to be instructed in the Universities, Colledges, or Schools, nor of the sick or poor into Hospitals, sick houses or publick Almshouses.

23. Those of the Reformed Religion shall be obliged to observe the Laws of the Catholick Church, received in this our Kingdom, as to Marriages and Contracts, and to contract in the degrees of consanguinity and affinity.

24. In like manner those of the said Religion shall pay the rights of Entry, as is accustomed for Offices unto which they shall be chosen, without being constrained to observe or assist in any Ceremonies contrary to their said Religion: and being called to take an Oath, shall not be obliged to do it otherwise than by holding up the hand, swearing and promising in the name of God, to say all the truth: Nor shall they be dispensed with for the Oath bv them taken in passing contracts and obligations.

25. We Will and Ordain, that all those of the Reformed Religion, and others who have followed their party, of what State, Quality or Condition soever they be, shall be obliged and constrained by all due and reasonable wayes, and under the penalties contained in the said Edict or Statute relating thereunto, to pay tythes to the Curates, and other Ecclesiasticks, and to all others to whom they shall appertain, according to the usage and custom of the places.

26. Disinheritations or Privations, be it in disposition in life-time or Testimentary, made from hatred only, or for Religion sake, shall have no place neither for the time passed or to come among our Subjects.

27. To the end to re-unite so much the better the minds and good will of our Subjects, as is our intention, and to take away all complaints for the future; We declare all those who make or shall make profession of the said Reformed Religion, to be capable of holding and exercising all Estates, Dignities, Offices, and publick charges whatsoever, Royal, Signorial, or of Cities of our Kingdom, Countreys, Lands and Lordships under our obedience, notwithstanding all Oaths to the contrary, and to be indifferently admitted and received into the same, and our Court of Parliament

and other Judges shall content themselves with informing and inquiring after the lives, manners, Religion and honest Conversation of those that were or shall be preferred to such offices, as well of the one Religion as the other, without taking other Oath of them than for the good and faithful service of the King in the exercise of their Office, and to keep the Ordinances, as they have been observed in all times. Also vacancies hapning of such of the said Estates, Charges, and offices as shall be in our disposition, they shall be provided by us indifferently, and without distinction of Persons, as that which tends to the Union of our Subjects. Understanding likewise that those of the Reformed Religion may be admitted and received into all Councells, Deliberations, Assemblies, and Functions depending upon the abovesaid things, without being rejected or hindred the injoynment thereof by reason of the said Religion.

28. We ordain for the interrment of the dead of the said Religion throughout the Cities and places of this Kingdom, that there shall in each place be provided for them by our Officers and Magistrates, and by the Commissioners that we shall depute for the execution of our present Edict or Statute, a place the most Commodious that can be: and the burying places which they have had heretofore, and whereof they have by the troubles been deprived, shall be restored unto them, except they be found to be converted into buildings of what quality or kind soever it be, in which case a compensation shall be made another way.

29. We enjoyn most expresly our officers to look to it, that no scandal be given in the said interrments, and they shall be obliged within fifteen days after request made, to provide those of the said Religion with convenient places for sepulchres, without delay, upon penalty of five hundred Crowns in their own proper and private names. And it is also forbidden, as well to the said officers as to all others, to exact any thing for the conduct of the said dead bodies upon penalty of Extortion.

30. To the end that Justice be given and administered to our Subjects, without any suspicion, hatred or favour, as being one of the principal means for the maintaining Peace and Concord, we have ordained and do ordain, that in our Court of Parliament of *Paris* shall be established a Chamber, composed of a President and sixteen Councellors of the said Parliament, which shall be called and entituled the Chamber of Edict, and shall take cognisance not only of the Causes and Process of

those of the said Reformed Religion which shall be within the jurisdiction of the said Court; but also of the Appeals of our Parliaments of *Normandie* and *Bretagne*, according to the jurisdiction which shall be hereafter given to it by this present Edict or Statute, and that until in each of the said Parliaments, there shall be established a Chamber for rendring Justice upon the place. We ordain also, That of four Offices of councellors in our said Parliament, remaining of the last erection which hath by us been made, there shall be presently provided and received in the said Parliament, four of the said Reformed Religion sufficient and capable, which shall be distributed; (to wit) the first into the Chamber of Edicts, and the other three in like manner shall be received in the three Chambers of Inquests; and besides, the two first Offices of Councellors of the said Courts, which shall come to be vacant by death, shall be supplied by two of the Reformed Religion, and the same distributed also in the two other Chambers of Inquests.

31. Besides the Chamber heretofore established at *Castres*, for Appeals from our Parliament of *Tholouse*, which shall be continued in the Estate it is, we have for the same reasons ordained, that in each of our Parliaments of *Grenoble* and *Bordeaux*, there shall be in like manner established a Chamber, composed of two Presidents, one a *Catholick*, and the other of the Reformed Religion, and twelve Councellors, whereof six shall be *Catholicks*, and the other six of the said Religion; which *Catholick* President and Councellors shall be by us chosen and taken out of the body of our said Courts. And as to those of the Religion, there shall be made a new Creation of one President and six Counsellors for the Parliament of *Bordeaux*, and one President and three Councellors for that of *Grenoble*, which with the three Councellors of the said Religion which are at present in the said Parliament, shall be imployed in the said Chamber of *Dauphine*. And the said Officers shall be created by a new Creation, with the same Salleries, Honours, Authorities, and Preheminences, as the others of the said Courts. And the said seat of the said Chamber of *Bordeaux* shall be in the said City of *Bordeaux*, or at *Nerat*, and that of *Dauphine* at *Grenoble*.

32. The Chamber of *Dauphine* shall take Cognizance of the Causes of those of the Reformed Religion within the jurisdiction of our Parliament of *Province*, without having need of Letters of Evocation, or Appeal, or other Provisions, than in our Chancery of *Dauphine*. As also those of the said Religion of *Normandy* and *Brittan*

shall not be obliged to take Letters of Evocation or Appeal, nor other Provision than in our Chancery of *Paris*.

33. Our Subjects of the Reformed Religion of the Parliament of *Burgundy*, shall have the choice to Plead in the Chamber ordained in the Parliament of *Paris*, or in those of *Dauphine*, and shall not be obliged to take Letters of Evocation of Appeal nor other Provisions than in the said chanceries of *Paris* or *Dauphine*, according as they shall make choice.

34. All the said several Chambers composed as is said, shall have Cognisance, and by decree shall Judge in Soveraignty and last Appeal, exclusive to all others, the Process and differences that are already, or shall arise, in which those of the Reformed Religion are or shall be Parties, Principalls or Guarrantees, in demanding or defending in all matters as well Civil as Criminal, if demanded before contestation in the Cause, and commencing of the Suit: whether the Process be by writing or verbal Appellation; excepting nevertheless all customs belonging to Benefices and the possessors of tenths, not infeoffed, the Ecclesiastical Patrons and their suits for their rights and duties, and the demains of the Church; all which shall be tryed and Judged in the Courts of Parliament exclusive to the said Chambers of Edict. As also we will and require that as to judging and deciding the Criminal Process which may happen betwixt the said Ecclesiasticks and those of the Reformed Religion, that if the Ecclesiasticks are defendant in such case, Recognizance and Judgment of criminal Process shall belong to our Soveraign courts distinct as to the said Chamber; and where the Ecclesiasticks shall be Plaintiff, and one of the Reformed Religion Defendant, the Cognizance and Judgment of Criminal Process shall belong in last Appeal to the said Chambers established. And we acknowledge also the said Chambers in time of Vacations for matters attributed by the Edicts and Ordinances to belong to the said Chambers established for times of Vacation, each within his Jurisdiction.

35. The Chamber of *Grenoble* shall be from henceforward united and incorporated into the body of the said Court of Parliament, and the President and Councellors of the Reformed Religion shall be called President and Councellors of the said Court, and hold the rank and number of the same, and to this end shall be first distributed through the other Chambers, and then drawn from them to be imployed and serve in that which we now ordain of new, with condition nevertheless, that they

shall assist and have voice and session in all the deliberations which the Chamber assembled shall have, and shall enjoy the same Sallary, authority and preheminence which the other Presidents and Counsellors of the said Courts do enjoy.

36. We will and ordain, that the said Chamber of *Castres* and *Bourdeaux* be united and incorporated in the same Parliaments, in the same manner and form as others: and when need shall require, and that the Causes which have moved us to make this establishment shall cease, and shall not have any more place among our Subjects; then shall the Presidents and Councellors of the same, of the said Reformed Religion, be held for Presidents and Councellors of the said Courts.

37. There shall also be a new creation or erection in the Chamber ordained in the Parliament of *Bourdeaux*, of two substitutes for our Procurators, or Attorneys and Advocates Generall, whereof one shall be Catholick, and the other of the Reformed Religion, which shall have the said Offices with competent Sallaries.

38. The substitutes shall not assume other qualities than that of substitutes; and when the Chambers or Courts ordained for the Parliaments of *Tholouse* and *Bourdeaux,* shall be united and incorporated to the said Parliaments, the said Substitutes shall have the Office of Councellors in the same.

39. The dispatches of the Chancery of *Bourdeaux* shall be perused in the presence of two Councellors of the same Chamber, whereof one shall be a Catholick, and the other of the Reformed Religion. In the absence of one of the Masters of Request of our Pallace, one of the Notaries and Secretaries of the said Court of Parliament of *Bourdeaux*, shall be Resident in the place where the said Chamber shall be established, or else one of the ordinary Secretaries of the Chancery to sign the dispatches of the said Chancery.

40. We will and ordain, that in the said Chamber of *Bourdeaux*, there shall be two Commissioners of the Register of the said Parliament, the one Civil and the other Criminal, who shall exercise their Offices by our Commissions, and shall be called Commissioners to the Register Civil and Criminal; but nevertheless shall not be revoked by the Registers of the Parliament, yet shall be accountable for the profits of the Offices to the said Registers, which Commissioners shall be Sallaried by the said

Registers as the said Chamber shall think fit to appoint, there shall be ordained some Catholick Messengers, who shall be taken in the said Court or elsewhere, according to our pleasure; besides which, there shall also be two *de novo* freely chosen of the Reformed Religion: And all the said Messengers, or Door-keepers shall be regulated by the said Chamber or court, as well in the exercise of their Offices as in the Profits or Fees which they shall take. There shall also be a Commission dispatched for payment of Sallaries and receiving of Amerciaments of the said court, which shall be such as we shall please to appoint. If the said Chamber shall be established in other place than the said City, the Commission heretofore agreed for paying the Sallaries of the Chamber of *Castres*, shall go out in its full and intire effect, and there shall be joyned to the said Office, the Commission for the receipt of the Amerciaments of the said Court.

41. There shall be provided good and sufficient assignations for the Sallaries of the Officers of the Chambers ordained by this Edict.

42. The Presidents, Councellors, and other Catholick Officers of the said Chambers or Courts, shall be continued so long as we shall see it to be for our service, and the good of our Subjects: And in the dismissing any of them others shall be admitted in their places, before their departure, they having no power during their Service to depart, or be absent from the said Chambers, without the leave of the same, which shall be judged of according to the Ordinance.

43. The said Chambers or Courts *Myparties* shall be established within six months, during which (if the establishment shall be so long in doing) the Process commenced, and to be commenced, where those of the Religion shall be parties within the jurisdiction of our Parliaments of *Paris, Rouen, Dijon* and *Rennes*, shall be presently removed to the Chamber or Court established at *Paris*, by vertue of the Edict of 1577. or else to the great Councell at their Election, and those which shall be of the Parliament of *Bourdeaux*, to the Chamber or Court established at *Castres*, or to the said grand Councell at their Election, and those which shall be of *Provence*, to the Parliament of *Grenoble*. And if the said Chambers, or Courts, are not established within three Months after the presentation of our Edict that Parliament which shall make refusal thereof, shall be prohibited the Cognizance and Judgement of the causes of those of the Religion.

44. The Process not yet judged, depending in the said Courts of Parliaments and great Counsel of the quality abovesaid, shall be sent back in what Estate soever they be, to the said Chambers or Courts, each within his jurisdiction, if one of the Parties of the Religion require it within four Months after the Establishment of the same; and as to those which shall be discontinued, and are not in condition of being judged, those of the said religion shall be obliged to make Declaration upon the first intimation and signification to them of the Prosecution, and the time past shall not be understood to require the dismission.

45. The said Chambers (or Courts) of *Grenoble* and *Bourdeaux*, as also that of *Castres*, shall keep the forms and stile of Parliaments, where the jurisdiction of the same shall be established, and shall judge by equal numbers of the one and the other Religion, if the Parties consent not to the Contrary.

46. All the Judges to whom the Address shall be made for execution of Decrees, Commissions of the said Chambers, and Patents obtained in Chancery for the same, together with all the Messengers and Serjeants, shall be obliged to put them in execution, and the said Messengers and Serjeants shall do all Acts throughout our Kingdom, without demanding a Placet, or peremptory Warrant, upon penalty of suspension of their Estates, and of the expenses, damages, and interests of the Parties, the Cognizance whereof shall belong to the said Chambers.

47. No removal of Causes shall be allowed to any whereof the Cognizance is attributed to the said Chambers, except in cases of Ordinance, the removal by which shall be made to the next Chamber established according to our Edict. And the dividing of the Process of the same Chambers shall be judged by the nearest, observing the proportion and forms of the same Chambers, where the Process shall be proceeded upon; except the Chamber of Edict in our Parliament of *Paris*, where the Process divided shall be distributed in the same Chamber by the Judges, which shall be by us named by our particular Letters Patent for that effect, if the parties had not rather wait the removing of the said Chamber. And happening that one and the same Process be divided in all the Chambers, *Myparties*, or half on Religion, half th'other, the division shall be sent to the Chamber of *Paris*.

48. The refusal that shall be proposed against the Presidents and Councellors of the Chambers, half of one Religion and half the other, called the Court of Edict, may be judged by the number of six, to which number the parties shall be obliged to restrain themselves, otherwise they shall be passed over without having regard to the said Refusal.

49. The examinations of the Presidents and Councellors newly erected in the Chambers of Edict, *Myparties*, shall be made in our Privy Council, or by the said Chambers each in his Precinct, when they shall be a sufficient number; and nevertheless the Oath accustomed shall be by them taken in the Courts where the said Chambers shall be established, and upon refusal, in our Privy Council: except those of the Chamber of *Languedoc,* in which they shall take Oath before our Chancellor, or in the same Chamber.

50. We Will and Ordain, That the reception of our Officers of the said Religion, judged in the said Chambers half Papist and half of the Reformed Religion by Pluralities of Voices, as is accustomed in other Courts, without being needfull that the opinions surpass two thirds, following the ordinance which for the same cause is abrogated.

51. There shall be made in the said Chambers *Myparties*, the Propositions, Deliberations, and Resolutions which shall appertain to the publick Peace, and for the particular State and Policy of the Cities where the same Chambers shall be.

52. The Article for the jurisdiction of the said Chambers ordained by the present Edict, shall be followed and observed according to its form and tenure, even in that which concerns the execution or breach of our Edict, when those of the Religion shall be Parties.

53. The Kings subordinate Officers, or others whereof the reception belongeth to our Courts of Parliament, if they be of the Reformed Religion, they may be examined and received in the said Chambers, *viz* those under the jurisdiction of the Parliaments of *Paris, Normandy* and *Bretagne*, in the said Chambers of *Paris*; those of *Dauphine* and *Provence*, in the Chamber of *Grenoble*; those of *Burgundy* in the said Chamber of *Paris*, or *Dauphine*, at their choice; those under the jurisdiction of

Thoulouse, in the Chamber of *Castres*; and those of the Parliament of *Bourdeaux*, in the Chamber of *Guyenne*; without that others may oppose themselves against their reception; and render themselves Parties, as our procurators General and their Substitutes, and those enjoying the said Offices: Yet nevertheless the accustomed Oath shall be by them taken in the Courts of Parliaments, who shall not take any Cognizance of the said receptions; and in refusal of the said Parliaments, the said Officers shall take the Oath in the said Chambers; after which so taken, they shall be obliged to present by a Messenger or Notary, the Act of their reception, to the Register of the said Courts of Parliaments, and to leave a coppy thereof examined by the said Register, who is enjoyned to Register the said Acts, upon penalty of all the expence, dammage and interest of the Parties; and the Registers refusing to do it, shall suffer the said Offices to report the Act of the said Summons, dispatched by the said Messengers or Notaries, and cause the same to be Registered in the Register-Office of their said Jurisdiction, for to have recourse thereunto when need shall be, upon penalty of Nullity of their proceedings and Judgements. And as to the Officers, whereof the reception hath not been accustomed to be made in our said Parliaments, in case those to whom it belongs shall refuse to proceed to the said examination and reception, then the said Officers shall repair to the said Chambers for to be there provided as it shall appertain.

54. The Officers of the said Reformed Religion, who shall hereafter be appointed to serve in the body of our said Courts of Parliaments, grand Counsell, Chambers of Accompts, Courts of Aids, Officers of the general Treasuries of *France*, and other Officers of the Exchequer, shall be examined and received in places where they have been accustomed, and in case of refusal or denying of Justice, they shall be appointed by our Privy Council.

55. The reception of our Officers made in the Chamber heretofore established at *Castres*, shall remain valid notwithstanding all Decrees and Ordinances to the contrary. And shall be also valid, the reception of Judges, Councellors, Assistants, and other Officers of the said Religion made in our Privy Council, or by Commissioners by us ordained in case of the refusal of our Courts of Parliaments, Courts of Aids, and Chambers of Accompts, even as if they were done in the said Courts and chambers, and by the other Judges to whom the reception belongeth. And their Sallaries shall be allowed them by the Chambers of Accompt without difficulty; and

if any have been put out, they shall be established without need of any other command than the present Edict, and without that the said Officer shall be obliged to shew any other reception, notwithstanding all Decrees given to the contrary which shall remain null and of none effect.

56. In the mean time untill the charges of the Justice of the said Chambers can be defrayed by Amerciaments, there shall be provided by us by valuable assignations sufficient for maintaining the said charges, without expecting to do it by the Goods of the Condemned.

57. The Presidents and Councellors of the Reformed Religion heretofore received in our Court of Parliament of *Dauphine*, and in the Chamber of Edict incorporated in the same, shall continue and have their Session and Orders for the same; that is to say, Presidents, as they have injoyed, and do injoy at present, and the Councellors according to the Decrees and Provisions that they have heretofore obteined in our Privy Council.

58. We declare all Sentences, Judgements, Procedures, Seisures, Sales, and Decrees made and given against those of the Reformed Religion, as well living as dead, from the death of the deceased King *Henry* the Second our most honoured Lord and Father in Law, upon the occasion of the said Religion, Tumults and Troubles since hapning, as also the execution of the same Judgments and Decrees, from henceforward cancelled, revoked, and anulled. And we ordain, that they shall be eased and taken out of the Registers Office of the Court, as well Soveraign as inferiour: And we Will and Require also to be taken away and defaced all Marks, Foot-steps, and Monuments of the said Executions, Books, and other Acts defamatory against their Persons, Memory and Posterity, and that the places which have been for that occasion demolished or rased, be rendred in such condition as now they are to the Proprietors of the same, to enjoy and dispose at their pleasure. And generally we cancell, revoke and null all proceedings and informations made for any enterprize whatsoever, pretended Crimes of High Treason, and others: notwithstanding the procedures, decrees and judgements containing re-union, incorporation, and confiscation; and we farther Will and Command, that those of the Reformed Religion, and others that have followed their party, and their Heirs re-enter really and actually into the possession of all and each of their Goods.

59. All Proceedings, Judgements and Decrees given, during the troubles against those of the Religion who have born Arms, or are retired out of our Kingdom, or within the same into Cities and Countries by them held, or for any other cause as well as for Religion and the troubles; together with all non-suiting of Causes, Prescriptions, as well Legal, Conditional, as Customary, seizing of Fiefs fallen during the troubles, by hindring Legitimate proceedings, shall be esteemed as not done or happening; and such we have declared and do declare, and the same we have and do annihilate and make void, without admitting any satisfaction thereof: but they shall be restored to their former condition, notwithstanding the decrees and execution of the same; and the possession thereof shall be rendred to them, out of which they were upon this account disseised. And this, as above, shall have like place, upon the account of those that have followed the party of those of the Religion, or who have been absent from our Kingdom upon the occasion of the troubles. And for young children of persons of Quality abovesaid, who died during the troubles, We restore the parties into the same condition as they were formerly, without refunding the expence, or being obliged for the Amerciaments not understanding nevertheless that the Judgements given by the chief Judges, or other inferiour Judges against those of the Religion, or who have followed their Party, shall remain null, if they have been given by Judges sitting in Cities by them held, which was to them of free access.

60. The Decrees given in our Court of Parliament, in matters whereof the Cognizance belongs to the Chambers or Courts ordained by the Edict in the year 1577 and Articles of *Nerac* and *Flex* into which Courts the Parties have not proceeded voluntarily, but have been forced to alledge and propose declinatory ends, and which decrees have been given by default or foreclusion, as well in Civil as Criminal matters, notwithstanding which Allegations the said Parties have been constrained to go on, shall be in like manner null and of no value. And as to the decrees given against those of the Religion, who have proceeded voluntarily, and without having proposed ends declinatory, those decrees shall remain without prejudice for the execution of the same. Yet nevertheless permitting them, if it seem good to them, to bring by Petition their Cause before the Chamber ordained by the present Edict, without that the elapsing the time appointed by the Ordinances shall be to their prejudice: and untill the said Chambers and Chanceries, for the same shall be established. Verbal appellations, or in writing interposed by those of the Religion before Judges, Registers, or

Commissioners, Executors of Decrees and Judgements, shall have like effect as if they were by command from the King.

61. In all inquiries which shall be made for what cause soever in matters Civil, if the Inquisitor or Commissioner be a Catholick, the Parties shall be obliged to convene an Assistant, and where they will not do it, there shall be taken from the Office by the said Inquisitor or Commissioner one who shall be of the Religion, and the same shall be practiced when the Commissioner or Inquisitor shall be of the said Religion for an Assistant who shall be a Catholick.

62. We Will and Ordain, That our Judges may take Cognizance of the validity of Testaments, in which those of the Religion may have an interest if they require it; and the appellations from the said Judgements, may be brought to the said Chambers ordained for the Process of those of the Religion; notwithstanding all Customs to the contrary, even those of *Bretagne*.

63. To obviate all differences which may arise betwixt our Courts of Parliaments, and the Chambers of the same Courts, ordained by the present Edict, there shall be made by us a good and ample Reglement, betwixt the said Courts and Chambers, and such as those of the Religion shall enjoy entirely from the said Edict, the which Reglement shall be verified in our Courts of Parliaments, and kept and observed without having regard to precedents.

64. We inhibit and forbid all our Courts, Soveraign and others of this Realm, the taking of Cognizance, and judging the Civil, or Criminal process of those of the Religion; the Cognizance of which is attributed by our Edict to the Chambers of Edict; provided that the Appeal thereunto be demanded as is said in the Fortieth Article going before.

65. We also Will and Command, for the present, and untill we have otherwise therein ordained, that in all Process commenced, or to be commenced where those of the Religion are Plaintiff or Defendants, Parties, Principals or Guarantees in matters Civil, in which our Officers and chief Courts of Justice have power to judge without appeal, that it shall be permitted to them to except against two of the Chamber, where the Process ought to be Judged, who shall forbear Judgement of the same; and

without having the cause expressed, shall be obliged to withdraw, notwithstanding the ordinance by which the Judges ought not to be accepted against without cause shown, and shall have farther right to except against others upon shewing cause. And in matters Criminal, in which also the said Courts of Justice and others of the Kings subordinate Judges do Judge without appeal, those of the Religion may except against three of the said Judges without shewing Cause. And the Provosts of the Marshalsies of *France*, vice-Bayliffs, vice-Presidents, Lievtenants of the short Robe, and other Officers of the like Quality shall Judge according to the Ordinances and Reglements heretofore given upon the account of Vagabonds. And as to the household charged and accused by the Provosts, if they are of the said Religion, they may require that three of the said judges, who might have Cognizance thereof, do abstain from the Judgement of their Process, and they shall be obliged to abstain therefrom without having cause shewn except where the Process is to be judged, there shall be found to the number of two in Civil, and three in Criminal Causes of the Religion, in which case it shall not be lawfull to except without Cause shewn: and this shall be reciprocall in the like cases, as above, to the Catholicks upon the account of Appeals from the Judges, where those of the Religion are the greater number, not understanding nevertheless that the chief Justice, Provosts of the Marshalsies, vice-Bayliffs, vice-Stewards, and others who judge without appeal, take by virtue of this that is said, Cognizance of the past Troubles. And as to crimes and excess happening by other occasions than the troubles since the beginning of *March*, 1585. untill the end of 1597. in case they take Cognizance thereof, We will that an appeal be suffered from their Judgement to the Chamber ordained by the present Edict, as shall be practiced in like manner for the Catholick and Confederates, where those of the Religion are Parties.

66. We Will and Ordain also, that henceforward in all instructions other than informations of criminal Process in the chief Justices Court of *Tholouse, Carcassonne, Roverque, Loragais, Beziers, Montpellier and Nimes*, the Magistrate or Commissary deputed for the said instructions if he is a Catholick shall be obliged to take an Associate who is of the Religion, whereof the Parties shall agree; or where they cannot agree, one of the Office of the said Religion shall be taken by the abovesaid Magistrate or Commissioner: as in like manner, if the said Magistrate or

Commisioner is of the Religion, he shall be obliged in the same manner, as abovesaid, to take and associate a Catholick.

67. When it shall be a question of making a criminal Process by the Provosts of the Marshalsies or their Leivetenants, against some of the Religion, a house-keeper who is charged and accused of a crime belonging to the Provost, or subject to the Jurisdiction of a Provost, the said Provost or their Leivetenants, if they are Catholicks, shall be obliged to call to the instruction of the said Process an Associate of the Religion: which Associate shall also assist at the Judgement of the difference, and in the definitive Judgement of the said Process: which difference shall not be judged otherwise than by the next Presidial Court assembled with the principal Officers of the said Court which shall be found upon the place, upon penalty of nullity, except the accused shall require to have the difference Judged in the Chambers ordained by the present Edict: In which case upon the account of the house-keepers in the Provinces of *Guyenne, Languedoc, Province,* and *Dauphine,* the substitutes of our Procurators general in the said Chambers, shall at the request of the said house-keepers, cause to be brought into the same the Charges and Informations made against them, to know and judge if the Causes are tryable before the Provost or not, that according to the quality of the crimes they may by the Chamber be sent back to the Ordinary, or judged tryable by the Provost, as shall be found reasonable by the contents of our present Edict; and the Presidial Judges, Provosts of Mareschalsie, vice-Bayliffs, vice-Stewards, and others who Judge without Appeal, shall be obliged respectively to obey and satisfie the commands of the said Chambers, as they use to do to the said Parliaments, upon Penalty of the loss of their Estates.

68. The outcries for sale of Inheritances, and giving notice therof by warning passed or chalked according to order, shall be done in places and at hours usual, if possible, following our Ordinances, or else in publick Markets, if in the place where the Land lies there is a Market-place; and where there shall be none in the next Market within the jurisdiction of the Court where Judgement ought to be given: and the fixing of the notice shall be upon the posts of the said Market-place, and at the entry of the Assembly of the said place, and this order being observed, the notice shall be valid, and pass beyond the interposition of the sentence or decree, as to any nullity which might be alleged upon this account.

69. All Titles and papers, instructions, and documents which have been taken, shall be restored by both parties to those to whom they belong, though the said Papers, or the Castles and houses in which they were kept, have been taken and seized by special Commission from the late deceased King, our most honoured Lord and Brother in Law, or from us, or by the command of the Governors and Lievetenant Generals of our Provinces, or by the authority of the heads of the other party, or under what pretext soever it shall be.

70. The children of those that are retired out of our Kingdom since the death of *Henry* the Second our Father in Law, by reason of Religion and Troubles, though the said Children are born out of the Kingdom, shall be held for true French Inhabitants: And we have declared and do declare, that it is Lawful for such as at any time within ten years after the publication of this present Edict, to come and dwell in this Kingdom without being needfull to take Letters Patents of Naturalization, or any other provision from us than this present Edict, notwithstanding all Ordinances to the contrary touching Children born in Foraign Countreys.

71. Those of the Reformed Religion, and all others who have followed their Party, who have before the troubles taken to farm any Office, or other Domaine, Gabel, Foraign Imposition, or other rights appertaining unto us, which they could not enjoy by reason of the troubles, shall remain discharged, and we discharge them of what they have not received of our Finances, and of what they have without fraud paid otherwise than into the receipts of our Exchequer, notwithstanding all their obligation given thereupon.

72. All places, Cities, and profits of our Kingdom, Countries, Lands and Lordships under our obedience, shall use and enjoy the same Priviledges, Immunities, Liberties, Franchises, Fairs, Markets, Jurisdictions and Courts of Justice which they did before the troubles began in 1585. and others preceeding, notwithstanding all Patents to the contrary, and translation of any of the Seals of Justice, provided they have been done only by occasion of the troubles, which Courts or Seats of Justice shall be restored to the Cities and places where they have been formerly.

73. If there are any Prisoners who are yet kept by authority of Justice, or otherwise, in Gallies, by reason of the Troubles, or of the said Religion, they shall be released and set in full Liberty.

74. Those of the Religion shall never hereafter be charged and oppressed with any charge ordinary or extraordinary more than the Catholicks, and according to their abilities and trades; and the parties who shall pretend to be over-charged above their abilities may appeal to the Judges, to whom the Cognizance belongs, and all our Subjects as well Catholick as of the Reformed Religion, shall be indifferently discharged of all charge which have been imposed by one and the other part, during the troubles, upon those that were on the contrary party, and not consenting, as also of debts created and not paid, the expences made without consent of the same, *without nevertheless having power to recover the revennue which should have been imployed to the payment of the said Charges.*

75. We do not also understand, that those of the Religion, and others who have followed their party, nor the Catholicks who dwell in Cities and places kept and imployed by them, and who have contributed to them, shall be prosecuted for the payment of Tailles, Aids, Grants, Fifteens, Taillon, Utensils, Reparations, and other impositions and subsidies fallen due and imposed during the troubles hapning before and untill our coming to the Crown, be it by Edicts, commands of deceased Kings our Predecessors, or by the advice and deliberation of Governors and Estates of Provinces, Courts of Parliament, and others, whereof we have discharged and do discharge them, prohibiting the Treasurers-General of *France* and of our Finances, Receivers General and Particular, their Commissioners and Agents, and other Intendants and Commissaries of our said Finances, to prosecute them, molest, disquiet, directly or indirectly, in any kind whatsoever.

76. All Generals, Lords, Knights, Gentlemen, Officers, Common-Councills of Cities and Commonalities;[4] and all others who have aided and succoured them, their Wives, Heirs, and Successors, shall remain quitted and discharged of all Money which have been by them and their order taken and levied, as well as the Kings Money, to what sum soever it may amount, as of Cities and Communities, and par-

---

[4] "Corps de villes et communautez."

ticular rents, revennues, plate, sale of moveable goods, Ecclesiastick, and other Woods of a high growth, be it of Domains or otherwise, Amerciaments, Booty, Ransoms, or other kind of Money taken by them, occasioned by the troubles began in the month of *March*, 1585. and other precedent troubles, untill our coming to the Crown, so that they or those that have by them been imployed in the levying of the said money, or that they have given or furnished by their Orders, shall not be therefore any wayes prosecuted at present, or for the time to come: and shall remain acquitted as well themselves, as their Commissaries, for the management and administration of the said Money, expecting all thereof discharged within four months after the publication of the present Edict made in our Parliament of *Paris*, acquittances being duly dispatched for the Heads of those of the Religion, or for those that had been commissioned for the auditing and ballancing of the Accounts, or for the Communities of Cities who have had Command and Charge during the said troubles, and all the said Heads of the Reformed Religion, and others who have followed their party (as if they were particularly expressed and specified) since the death of *Henry* the Second our Father in Law, shall in like manner remain acquitted and discharged of all acts of hostility, leavies, and conduct of Soldiers, minting and valuing of Money (done by Order of the said chief Commanders) casting and taking of Ordnance and Ammunition, compounding of Powder and Salt-Peter, prizes, fortifications, dismantling and demolishing of Cities, Castles, Burroughs, and Villages, enterprises upon the same, burning and demolishing of Churches and Houses, establishing of Judicatures, Judgements, and Executions of the same, be it in Civil or Criminal matters, Policy and Reglement made amongst themselves, Voyages for intelligence, Negotiations, Treaties and Contracts made with all Foraign Princes and Communities, the introduction of the said strangers into Cities and other places, of our Kingdom, and generally of all that hath been done, executed and Negotiated during the said troubles, since as aforesaid, the death of *Henry* the Second our Father in Law.

77. Those of the said Religion shall also remain discharged of all General and Provincial assemblies by them made and held, as well at *Nantes* as since in other places untill this present time; as also of Councils by them established and ordained by Provinces, Declarations, Ordinances, and Reglements made by the said Assemblies and Councells, Establishing and Augmentations of Garrisons, assembling and taking of Soldiers, levying and taking of our Money, be it from the Receivers-general

or particular Collectors of Parishes, or otherwise in what manner soever, seizures of Salt, continuation or erection of Taxes, Tolls, and Receipts of the same at *Royan*, and upon the Rivers of *Charant, Garonne, Rosne,* and *Dordonne*, arming and fighting by Sea, and all accidents and Excess hapning upon forcing the payment of Taxes, Tolls, and other Money by fortifying of Cities, Castles, and places, impositions of Money and day-works, receipts of the same Money, displacing of our Receivers, Farmers, and other Officers, establishing others in their places, and of all Leagues, Dispatches and Negotiations made as well within as without the Kingdom: and in general, of all that hath been done, deliberated, written, and ordained by the said Assembly and Councell, so that those who have been given their advice, signed, executed, caused to sign and execute the said Ordinances, Reglements and deliberations, shall not be prosecuted, or their Wives, Heirs and Successors, now and for the time to come, though the particulars thereof be not amply declared. And above all, perpetual silence is hereby commanded to our Procurators-General and their Substitutes, and all those who may pretend to an interest therein, in whatsoever fashion or manner it may be, notwithstanding all Decrees, Sentences, Judgements, Informations, and Procedures made to the contrary.

78. We further approve, allow, and authorize the Accounts which have been heard, ballanced, and examined by the deputies of the said Assembly: willing and requiring that the same, together with the acquittances and pieces which have been rendred by the Accomptants, be carried into our Chambers of Accompts at *Paris*, three Months after the publication of this present Edict, and put into the hands of our Procurator-general, to be kept with the Books and Registers of our Chamber, to have there recourse to them as often as shall be needfull, and they shall not be subject to review, nor the Accomptants held in any kind liable to appearance or correction, except in the case of omission of receipts or false Acquittances: and we hereby impose silence upon our Procurator-generall, for the overplus that shall be found wanting, or for not observing of formalities: Prohibiting to our Accomptants, as well of *Paris* as of other Provinces where they are established, to take any Cognizance thereof in any sort or manner whatsoever.

79. And as the Accompts which have not yet been rendred, We Will and Ordain that the same be heard, ballanced and examined by the Commissaries, who shall by us be deputed thereunto, who without difficulty shall pass and allow all the parcels

paid by the said Accomptants, by vertue of the Ordinances of the said Assembly, or others having power.

80. All Collectors, Receivers, Farmers, and all others, shall remain well and duly discharged of all the sums of Money which have been paid to the said Commissioners of the Assembly, of what nature soever they be, untill the last day of this Month. And we will and command, that all be passed and allowed in the accompts, which Accompts they shall give into our Chambers of Accompts, purely and simply by vertue of the Acquittances which shall be brought; and if any shall hereafter be delivered they shall remain null, and those who shall accept or deliver them, shall be condemned in the penalty of Forgery. And where there shall be any Accompts already given in, upon which there shall have intervened any Raisings or Additions, we do hereby take away the same, and re-establish the parties intirely, by vertue of these presents, which being needfull to have particular Patents, or any other thing than an extract of this present Article.

81. The Governors, Captains, Consuls, and Persons Commissioned to recover Money for paying Garrisons held by those of the Religion, to whom our Receivers and Collectors of Parishes have furnished by Loan upon their credits and obligations, whether by constraint, or in obedience to the commandment of the Treasurers-General, and the Money necessary for the entertaining of the said Garrisons, untill the concurrence of the State which we dispatched in the beginning of 1596 and augmentations since agreed unto by us, shall be held acquitted and discharged of all which hath been paid for the effect abovesaid, though by the said Scedules and obligations no mention hath been thereof made, which shall be to them rendred as null. And to satisfie therein the Treasurers-general in each generality, the particular Treasurers of our Tallies shall give their acquaintances to the said Collectors; and the Receivers-general shall give their acquittances to the said Collectors; and the Receivers-general shall give their acquittances to the particular Receivers: and for the discharge of the Receivers general, the sums whereof they should have given account, as is said, shall be indorsed upon the Commissions levied by the Treasured of the expenses, under the name of Treasurers-General for the extraordinaries of our Wars, for the payment of the said Garrisons. And where the said Commissions shall not amount to as much as the establishment and augmentations of our Army did in 1596. We ordain that supply the same, there shall be dispatched new Commissions for what

is necessary for the discharge of our Accomptants, and restitution of the said Promises and Obligations, in such sort as there shall not for the time to come be any thing demanded thereof from those that shall have made them, and that all Patents of Ratifications which shall be necessary for the discharge of Accomptants, shall be dispatched by virtue of this present Article.

82. Those also of the said Religion shall depart and desist henceforward from all Practices, Negotiations, and Intelligences, as well within as without our Kingdom; and the said Assemblies and Counsels established within the Provinces, shall readily separate, and also all the Leagues and Associations made or to be made under what pretext soever, to the prejudice of our present Edict, shall be cancelled and annulled, ás we do cancell and annull them; prohibiting most expresly to all our Subjects to make henceforwards any Assesments or Leavy's of Money, Fortifications, Enrollments of men, Congregations and Assemblies of other than such as are permitted by our present Edict, and without Arms: And we do prohibit and forbid them to do the contrary upon the penalty of being severely punished as Contemners and Breakers of our Commands and Ordinances.

83. All Prizes which have been taken by Sea, during the Troubles, by vertue of the leave and allowance given, and those which have been made by Land, upon those of the contrary Party, and which have been Judged by the Judges and Commissioners of the Admiralty, or by the Heads of those of the Religion, or their Councell, shall remain extinguished under the benefit of our present Edict, without making any prosecution; the Captains or others who have made the said Prizes, their Securities, Judges, Officers, Wives and Heirs, shall not be prosecuted nor molested in any sort whatsoever, notwithstanding all the decrees of our Privy Council and Parliaments, of all Letters of Mart and seizures depending and not Judged of, We will and require that there be made a full and intire discharge of all Suits arising therefrom.

84. In like manner there shall not be any prosecution of those of the Religion for the oppositions and obstructions which they have given formerly, and since the troubles, in the execution of Decrees and Judgements given for the re-establishment of the Catholic Religion in divers places of this Kingdom.

114

85. And as to what hath been done, or taken during the Troubles out of the way of Hostility, or by Hostility against the Publick or particular rules of the Heads of Communalities of the Provinces which they commanded, there shall be not prosecution by the way of Justice.

86. Foreasmuch that whereas that which hath been done against the rules of one party or the other is indifferently excepted and reserved from the general abolition contained in our present Edict, and is liable to be inquired after or prosecuted, yet nevertheless no Soldier shall be troubled, whence may arise the renewing of troubles; and for this cause, We Will and Ordain, that execrable cases shall only be excepted out of the said abolition: as ravishing and forcing Women and Maids, Burnings, Murders, Robberies, Treachery, and lying in wait or ambush, out of the way of hostility, and for private revenge, against the duty of War, breaking of Pass-ports and Safeguards, with murders and Pillages without command from those of the Religion, or those that have followed the party of their Generals who have had authority over them, founded upon particular occasions which have moved them to ordain and command it.

87. We Ordain also, that punishment be inflicted for Crimes and offences committed betwixt persons of the same party, if Acts not commanded by the hands of one Party of the other by necessity of Law and Order of War. And as for the Leavying and exacting of Money, bearing of Arms, and other exploits of War done by private authority and without allowance, the parties guilty thereof shall be prosecuted by way of Justice.

88. The Cites dismantled during the troubles, may with our permission be re-edified and repaired by the Inhabitants at their Costs and Charges, and the provisions granted heretofore upon that account shall hold and have place.

89. We Ordain, and our Will and Pleasure is, that all Lords, Knights, Gentlemen, and others of what quality and condition soever of the Reformed Religion, and others who have followed their Party, shall enter and be effectually conserved in the enjoyment of all and each of their Goods, Rights, Titles, and Actions, notwithstanding the Judgements following thereupon during the said troubles, and

by reason of the same: which Decrees, Seizures, Judgements, and all that follow therupon, we have to this end declared, and do declare them null and of no value.

90. The acquisitions that those of the Reformed Religion, and others which have followed their Party, have made by the authority of the deceased Kings our predecessors or others, for the immovables belonging to the Church, shall not have any place or effect; but we ordain and our pleasure is, that the Ecclesiasticks enter immediately, and without delay be conserved in the possession and enjoyment really and actually of the said goods so alienated, without being obliged to pay the purchase-money which to this effect we have cancelled and revoked as null, without remedy for the Purchasers to have against the Generals, &c. by the authority of which the said goods have been sold. Yet nevertheless for the re-imbursement of the Money by them truly and without fraud disturbed, our Letters Patents of permission shall be dispatched to those of the Religion, to interpose and equalize bare sums of the said purchases cost, the Purchasers not being allowed to bring any action for their Damages and interest for want of enjoyment; but shall content themselves with the reimbursement of the Money by them furnished for the price of the acquisitions, accounting for the price of the fruits received, in case that the said Sale should be found to be made at an under rate.

91. To the end that as well our Justices and Officers as our other Subjects be clearly and with all certainty advertised of our Will and Intentions, and for taking away all ambiguity and doubt which may arise from the variety of former Edicts, Articles, secret Letters Patents, Declarations, Modifications, Restrictions, Interpretations, Decrees and Registers, as also all secrets as well as other deliberations heretofore by us or the Kings our predecessors, made in our Courts of Parliaments or otherwayes, concerning the said Reformed Religion, and the troubles hapning in our said Kingdom, we have declared and do hereby declare them to be of no value and effect: and as to the derogatory part therein contained, we have by this Edict abrogated, and we do abrogate, and from henceforward we cancell, revoke, and annull them. Declaring expresly that our Will and Pleasure is, that this our Edict be firmly and inviolably kept and observed as well by our Justices and Officers, as other Subjects, without hesitation, or having any regard at all to that which may be contrary or derogatory to the same.

92. And for the greater assurance of the keeping and observing what we herein desire, we Will and Ordain, and it is our pleasure, that all the Governors and Leiuetenants General of our Provinces, Bayliffs, Chief-Justices and other ordinary Judges of the Cities of our said Kingdom immediately after the receit of this same Edict, and do bind themselves by Oath to keep and cause to be kept and observed each in their district as shall also the Mayors, Sheriffs, principal Magistrates, Consuls, and Jurates of Cities either annual or perpetual. Enjoyning likewise our Bayliffs, chief Justices, or their Leiuetenants, and other Judges to make the principal inhabitants of the said Cities, as well of the one Religion as the other, to swear to the keeping and observing of this present Edict immediately after the publication thereof: And taking all those of the said Cities under our Protection, command that one and the other respectively shall either answer for the opposition that shall be made to this our said Edict within the said Cities by the Inhabitants thereof, or else to present and deliver over to Justice the said opposers.

We Will and Command our well beloved the people holding our Courts of Parliaments, Chambers of Accounts, and Courts of Aids, that immediately after the receipt of this present Edict they cause all things to cease, and upon penalty of Nullity of the Acts which they shall otherwise do, to take the like Oath as above, and to publish and Register our said Edict in our said Courts according to the form and tenure of the same, purely and simply, without using any Modifications, Restrictions, Declarations, or secret Registers, or expecting any other Order or Command from us: and we do require our Procurators-general to pursue immediately and without delay the said publication hereof.

We give in command to the People of our said Courts of Parliaments, Chambers of our Courts, and Courts of Aids, Bayliffs, Chief-Justices, Provosts and other our Justices and Officers to whom it appertains, and to their Leiuetenants, that they cause to be read, published, and Registered this our present Edict and Ordinance in their Courts and Jurisdictions, and the same keep punctually, and the contents of the same to cause to be injoyned and used fully and peaceably to all those to whom it shall belong, ceasing and making to cease all troubles and obstructions to the contrary, for such is our pleasure: and in witness hereof we have signed these presents with our own hand; and to the end to make it a thing firm and stable for ever, we have caused to put and indorse our Seal to the same. Given at *Nantes* in the Month of *April* in the year of Grace 1598. and of our reign the ninth   signed

HENRY.

And underneath, the King being in Council,

FORGET.

And on the other side,   VISA.

This VISA signifies the Lord Chancellors perusal.

Sealed with the Great Seal of Green-wax upon a red and green string of Silk.

Read, Published and Registred, the Kings Procurator or Attorney-General Hearing and Consenting to it in the Parliament of Paris, the 25th of February, 1599.

Signed,   VOYSIN.

Read, Published, and in-Registred the Chamber of Accompts, the Kings Procurator-General Hearing and Consenting, the last day of May, 1599.

Signed,   De la FONTAINE.

Read, Published, and Registred, the Kings Procurator-General hearing and consenting, at Paris in the Court of Aids the 30th of April, 1599.

Signed,   BERNARD.

SECRET ARTICLES*

1. The sixth article of the said edict concerning liberty of conscience and permission for all His Majesty's subjects to live and dwell in this kingdom, and in other countries owing him allegience, shall apply and be observed according to its form and content: this will also apply to ministers, teachers, and all others who are or shall be of the said reformed religion, whether inside or outside France; in other respects they will behave in the manner specified in the edict.

2. Those of the reformed religion shall not be obliged to contribute to the repair or building of churches, chapels and presbyteries, nor to the purchase of vestments, lights, the founding of bells, and consecrated bread, nor shall they contribute to religious brotherhoods or the renting of premises for housing priests or monks, and similar things, unless they are obliged to do so by endowments, foundations or other arrangements entered into by them, their ancestors or predecessors.

3. Nor will they be obliged to drape and decorate their house-fronts on the feast days when this is statutory: they will only be expected to allow the local authorities to do so, without having to make any contribution themselves.

4. Similarly when those of the reformed religion are sick or at the point of death, they will not be required to receive the ministrations of anyone of a different religion, except when they are serving a prison sentence etc. and they may be visited and consoled by their ministers without let or hindrance; as for those serving a sentence, the said minister may also visit and bring comfort to them, but without offering public prayers, except in those places where public worship is permitted them by the edict.

5. Those of the reformed religion shall be allowed to worship publicly in Pimpoul, and for Dieppe, in the Le Paulet suburb; these places, Pimpoul and Le Paulet, shall be created *lieux de bailliages*. As regards Sancerre, the said practice of worship shall continue as at present, but will only be established there on condition that the inhabitants make it clear that they have the consent of their seigneur which

*Reprinted by permission of Faber and Faber Ltd. From Roland Mousnier, *The Assassination of Henry IV*. Faber and Faber Ltd., 1973 (Originally published by Editions Gallimard, Paris, 1964).

will be procured by the commissioners whom His Majesty will depute to carry out the edict. Free public worship shall also be re-established in the town of Montagnac in Languedoc.

6. Concerning the article which mentions *bailliages*, the following declarations and concessions have been made: first, in order to establish the practice of the reformed religion in the two places granted in each *bailliage*, seneschalsy and 'government', those of the reformed religion shall name two towns in the suburbs places, by reason of strife, infection, or any other legitimate obstacle, other places shall be provided so long as this situation persists. Secondly, in the Picardy 'government', there will be only two towns in whose suburbs those of the said religion will be able to worship—two for all dependent *bailliages*, and named as above, in which to establish the practice of the reformed religion, in addition to the other places where it is already established.

7. Everything granted in the preceding article for the practice of the reformed religion in the *bailliages*, will also apply to the lands formerly belonging to the late Queen, His Majesty's mother-in-law, and the *bailliage* of Beaujolais.

8. In addition to the two places granted for the practice of the said religion in the special articles of 1577, in the islands of Marennes and Oleron, they will be granted two more for the greater convenience of the inhabitants: one for all the Marennes islands, and another for the island of Oleron.

9. The provisions granted by His Majesty for the practice of the said religion in the town of Metz, will produce their full and entire effect.

10. His Majesty fully expects the article XXVII of his edict, concerning the admission of adherents of the reformed religion to offices and dignities, to be princes, seigneurs, noblemen and Catholic towns to own his allegience; these will not have any adverse effect on those of the said religion except as regards the practice of worship. And their worship shall be regulated according to the provisions of the articles which follow and which will govern the instructions given to the commissioners His Majesty will depute to carry out his edict, according to its terms.

11. According to the terms of the edict made by His Majesty to obtain the submission of the duke of Guise, the reformed religion shall not be practised or established in the towns and suburbs of Rheims, Rocroy, Saint-Dizier, Guise, Joinville, Fîmes, and Moncornet in the Ardennes.

12. The same restrictions apply to the other localities, to the environs of the towns and fortified places where worship was forbidden by the edict of 1577.

13. To remove any ambiguity which might arise from the word 'environs', His Majesty declares that he referred to the places which are in the suburbs of the said towns, in which places the practice of the reformed religion cannot be established unless specifically allowed in the 1577 edict.

14. Considering that this latter edict allowed the general practice of the said worship in the feoffs possessed by those of the reformed religion, including the suburbs, His Majesty declares that the same permission is to be granted now, also in the feoffs in the suburb held by those of the said religion, according to the provisions in his edict given at Nantes.

15. According to the edict issued on the defeat of marshal La Châtre, there will be, in each of the *bailliages* of Orleans and Bourges, only one place per *bailliage* for the practice of the said religion, but it may nevertheless be continued in the places in which its continuance is permitted by the edict of Nantes.

16. Permission to preach in the feoffs will also be granted in these *bailliages*, in the form laid down by the edict of Nantes.

17. Similarly the edict issued when the marshal Bois-Dauphin was defeated shall be observed, and there shall be no worship in the towns, suburbs, and fortified places he brought to His Majesty's service; as for their environs and suburbs, the '77 edict shall apply, even in the enfeoffed houses, as is stated in the edict of Nantes.

18. The said religion shall not be practised in the towns, suburbs or château of Morlaix, in accordance with the edict issued when the town surrendered, and the '77 edict shall be observed throughout its administration area, even in the feoffs, according to the edict of Nantes.

19. As a result of the edict issued on the surrender of Quinpercorantin, the said religion shall not be practised throughout the diocese of Cornouaille.

20. In accordance with the edict issued when Beauvais surrendered, there may be no practice of the said religion in the said town of Beauvais, nor for three leagues' radius. But it may be established in the rest of the *bailliage*, in the places allowed by the '77 edict, even in the enfeoffed houses, as is laid down in the edict of Nantes.

21. Inasmuch as the edict issued upon the surrender of the late Admiral de Villars is only provisional, and until further pronouncement by the King, it is His Majesty's earnest desire that his edict of Nantes should nevertheless be observed in the towns and districts brought under his allegience by the said admiral, as for the other places in his kingdom.

22. As a result of the edict issued on the surrender of the duke of Joyeuse, the said religion cannot be practised in the town of Toulouse, its suburbs, or a radius of four leagues, or any nearer than the towns of Villemur, Caraman, and l'Isle-Jourdain.

23. Nor can worship be established in the towns of Alet, Fiac, Aurillac and Montesquieu, with the proviso that, if any adherents of the reformed religion should, in these towns, insist on having a place of worship, they would be allotted by the commissioners whom His Majesty will make responsible for carrying out the edict, or else by the local officials, a suitable and readily accessible place for each town, not further than a league's distance away.

24. The said worship may be established, according to the provisions of the edict of Nantes, within the jurisdiction of the Parlement of Toulouse, except for the *bailliages*, seneschalsies, and their jurisdiction, whose main centre has been brought under allegience to the King by the said duke of Joyeuse, in which case the '77 edict will apply; His Majesty nevertheless intends worship to continue in those places within the *bailliages* and seneschalsies where it was practised before surrender, and intends worship to be allowed in the enfeoffed houses in these *bailliages* and seneschalsies, as is laid down in the edict of Nantes.

25. The edict issued for the surrender of the town of Dijon shall be observed, and according to this edict there will be no other religion practised in this town and suburbs but the Catholic, apostolic, and Roman faith, or for a radius of four leagues.

26. There will be similar observance of the edict made upon the surrender of the duke of Mayenne, whereby there shall be no worship according to the reformed religion in the towns of Chalons, or for two leagues round Soissons, for a period of six years, beginning from January 1596; after this period the edict of Nantes will be in force there as elsewhere in the kingdom.

27. Those of the reformed religion, no matter what their social status, shall be allowed to inhabit, to come and go freely in the town of Lyons and other towns and fortified places in the Lyonnois region, despite all prohibitions made by the syndics and magistrates of the towns of Lyons, and confirmed by His Majesty.

28. Only one place in the *bailliage* for the practice of the said religion shall be designated in the entire seneschalsy of Poitiers, in addition to those where it is already established; as regards the feoffs, the edict of Nantes will be followed. This worship will be continued in the town of Chauvigny: and it may not be re-established in the towns of Agen or Périgueux, even though the terms of the '77 edict permit this.

29. There shall be only two localities in the *bailliage* for the practice of this religion in the whole area of Picardy, as has been stated above, and these two places cannot be given within the jurisdiction of the *bailliages* and areas reserved by the edicts drawn up to mark the reduction of Amiens, Péronne and Abbeville. However, the said worship may be held in enfeoffed houses, throughout the Picardy area, as is laid down in the edict of Nantes.

30. The said religion shall not be practised in the town or suburbs of Sens, and only one place of *bailliage* shall be designated for worship throughout the administrative area of the *bailliage*, provided this does not prejudice the permission granted for enfeoffed houses, which will apply according to the terms of the edict of Nantes.

31. Similarly, the said religion may not be practised in the town and suburb of Nantes, and no place of *bailliage* will be designated for the purpose within a radius

of three leagues from the town: worship may however be held in enfeoffed houses, as is provided by the edict of Nantes.

32. His Majesty fully intends his edict of Nantes to come into force immediately, as regards the practice of the said religion in those places where edicts and agreements made for the reduction of certain Catholic princes, seigneurs, noblemen and towns, had forbidden it for the time being until further notice. In places where worship was forbidden until a certain date, it must be allowed once the period has elapsed.

33. A place shall be provided for those of the reformed religion to serve the town, (*prévôté*) and viscounty (*vicomté*) of Paris at not more than five leagues' distance from that town, in which they can worship publicly.

34. In all those places in which public worship is allowed, the people may be summoned, even by the ringing of bells, and there shall be all the usual activities and functions necessary to the practice of this religion, or to the maintenance of discipline, such as the holding of consistories, colloquies and provincial and national synods with His Majesty's permission.

35. The ministers, elders and deacons of the said religion shall not be obliged to appear in a court of justice to give evidence, for matters revealed in their consistories, if these are censures, except in matters concerning the King's person or the preservation of his state.

36. Those of the said religion who live in country areas may go to worship in the towns and suburbs and other places where public worship is established. places where public worship is established.

37. Those of the said religion may not keep public schools except in the towns and places where they are allowed public worship; the provisions formerly granted them for the erection and upkeep of schools will if necessary be verified, and will operate completely and effectively.

38. Fathers professing the said religion may provide their children with whatever instructors they desire, and may substitute one or several by means of a testament, codicil or other declaration made in the presence of notaries, or written

and signed by their hand, provided the laws current in this kingdom, the local ordinances and customs, retain their force and virtue, as regards the provision of guardians, tutors and administrators.

39. As regards the marriages of priests and religious persons already contracted, His Majesty has no intention, for a variety of solid considerations, of proceeding against them or molesting them. He will instruct his procurator-general and other officers to regard the matter as closed. Nevertheless His Majesty declares that he expects that the children of such marriages shall inherit only the chattels, property acquired in common, or acquired real estate of their mothers and fathers, or in default of children, then the next of kin and nearest heirs shall inherit: and their testaments, donations, and other arrangements which have been or will be made by such persons, for the bestowal of the said chattels, property acquired in common or acquired real estate, are declared completely valid. However, His Majesty does not wish the said professed priests and nuns to be able to enter on any direct or collateral succession; they may only take the property which has been or will be left them by wills, donations or other arrangements, always excepting those left by direct and collateral succession; as for those who were professed before the age prescribed in the ordinances of Orleans and Blois, the question of succession shall be entirely governed by the terms of these ordinances, each one for the time to which they apply.

40. His Majesty does not wish those of the reformed religion who may have previously or may hereafter enter upon marriages in the third or fourth degree, to be molested on that account, nor does he wish the validity of these marriages brought in question; as for marriages which may already have been contracted in the second degree, or from the second to the third, between people of the said religion, they may, on application to His Majesty, be afforded such provisions as may be necessary to ensure that such people are not pursued or molested, or their children's inheritance disputed or called in question.

41. To judge of the validity of marriages made and contracted by those of the said religion, and to decide whether they are legal, if an adherent of the reformed religion is the defendant, the judge royal will take cognizance of the fact of the said marriage; when he is the plaintiff and the defendant a Catholic, cognizance will appertain to the ecclesiastical official and judge; if both parties are of the reformed

religion, cognizance will belong to the judges royal. His Majesty wishes, as regards these marriages, and any disputes arising from them, that the judges ecclesiastical and judges royal, together with the chambers set up by this edict, shall respectively take cognizance of them.

42. Donations and bequests made or to be made, whether by the last will and testament or *inter vivos*, for the upkeep of ministers, scholars, students and the poor of the said reformed religion, and for other pious causes, will be valid, and will have full effect, despite all judgements, decrees and other contrary provisions, but without prejudice to His Majesty's rights or anyone else's, should these same bequests and donations fall into mortmain: all actions and lawsuits necessary to the possession of such bequests, pious works, and other rights, whether in or out of the courts, may be undertaken by attorney on behalf of the corporate community of those of the said religion which may be concerned: and if it is found that there have been any previous arrangements made for these donations and bequests, other than what is prescribed in the said article, no claim to restitution shall lie, other than in kind.

43. His Majesty allows those of the said religion to assemble in the presence of the judge royal, and on his authority to raise from amongst themselves the sum of money deemed necessary, to be used to defray the expenses of their synods, and the upkeep of those entrusted with the conduct of their worship. This statement shall be given to the said judge royal, to keep: a copy of this statement shall be sent by the said judge every six months to His Majesty or his chancellor; and the taxes and imposts of these moneys shall be enforceable, despite any opposition or appeals whatever.

44. The ministers of the said religion shall be exempt from guard and sentinel duties, from billeting soldiers, and other imposition and collection of *tailles*, together with guardianship, trusteeship and commission to guard property seized on judical authority.

45. In the case of any burials of those of the said religion, which have already taken place in the cemeteries belonging to the Catholics, no matter in what locality or town, it is His Majesty's wish that no enquiries, alterations or legal enquiries be made, and his officers will be instructed to refrain from any such action. As regards

the city of Paris, apart from the two cemeteries at present used by those of the reformed religion, namely la Trinité and Saint-Germain, they shall be given a third place where burials from the suburbs of Saint-Honoré and Saint-Denis may conveniently take place.

46. The Catholic presidents and councillors who will serve in the chamber set up in the Paris Parlement, will be chosen by His Majesty from the list of parliamentary officers.

47. The councillors of the reformed religion who will serve in the said chamber will be present, if they see fit, at the proceedings which will be settled by the commissioners, and they shall have a deliberative vote, though they will not have a share in the moneys laid down as guarantee except on those occasions on which by the order and prerogative of their reception they are obliged to be present.

48. The most senior president of the *chambres mi-parties* will preside at the audience, and in his absence the second, and the proceedings shall be shared between the two presidents, either jointly or alternately, for a month or for a week at a time.

49. When the offices fall vacant which were held by those of the said religion in the said chambers of the edict, they shall be filled by capable persons who shall be vouched for by the synod or colloquy to which they belong, as being of the reformed religion and estimable people.

50. The pardon afforded to those of the said reformed religion in the LXXIVth article of the said edict, will apply to the stealing of all royal funds, whether by breaking open of coffers or any other means, even in the case of those who were in revolt along the banks of the Charente, although they had been drafted and assigned to private individuals.

51. Article XLIX of the secret articles made in 1577 concerning the town and archbishopric of Avignon and countship of Venice, together with the treaty made at Nimes, will be observed according to their form and content; and no letters of marque, by virtue of these articles and treaties, will be given except by letters patent from the King sealed with his great seal. However, those desirous of obtaining them may do so by virtue of this present article and without further authorization, in the

presence of the judges royal, who will ascertain the contraventions, denials of justice, and iniquity of judgements proposed by those who desire to obtain the said letters, and they will send them bearing a sealed letter containing their opinion to His Majesty, to be dealt with as he thinks fit and reasonable.

52. His Majesty desires the reinstatement of maitre Nicolas Grimoult and desires him to retain the title and possess the office of *lieutenant général criminel* in the *bailliage* of Alencon, despite the fact of his handing his resignation to maitre Jean Marguerit, despite the latter's accepting it and despite the fact that maitre Guillaume Bernard obtained the office of *lieutenant général, civil et criminel* at the siege of Exmes: and the decrees issued against this said Marguerit who resigned from the *conseil privé* during the civil strife, in the years 1586, 1587 and 1588, whereby maitre Nicolas Barbier is maintained in the rights and prerogatives of *lieutenant général ancien* to the said *bailliage*, and the said Bernard to the office of lieutenant at Exmes, are all quashed by His Majesty, for certain good reasons, has commanded the said Grimoult to repay within three months the said Barbier the sum he paid to the *parties casuelles* for the office of *lieutenant général civil et criminel* in the viscounty of Alencon, and also his fifty crowns' expenses: the matter shall be settled by the bailiff Le Perche or his lieutenant in Mortagne. Once the money has been repaid, even if the said Barbier is reluctant or slow in accepting it, His Majesty has forbidden the said Barbier and also the said Bernard, once this present article has been published, to continue to haod or exercise the said offices, on pain of being accused of forgery, and he installs the said Grimoult in these offices and the rights thereto appertaining. In consequence the cases pending in His Majesty's *conseil privé* between the said Grimoult, Barbier and Bernard, are now concluded and suppressed; His Majesty forbids the Parlements and all other persons to take cognizance of these cases and forbids those involved to institute proceedings. Moreover His Majesty has undertaken to reimburse the said Bernard one thousand crowns paid to the *parties casuelles* for this office, and sixty crowns *pro rata* of his expenses; His Majesty has, to this end, set in train a transfer of funds which shall be recovered at the expense of the said Grimoult at his early convenience.

53. His Majesty will write to his ambassadors to insist through legal channels that none of his subjects, even those of the reformed religion, shall be molested on conscientious grounds, or subjected to the Inquisition, and that they shall be free to

come and go, to live, do business and engage in trade, in all foreign countries or those allied or united with this crown, provided they do not offend against the administration of the countries they are visiting.

54. His Majesty does not wish any enquiry to be made into the method of raising taxes in Royan, by virtue of a contract entered into with the sieur de Candelay, and others subsequent to it, which approve and declare valid the said contract for the time during which it had applied in its entirety, up to the eighteenth day of next May.

55. The excesses committed by Armand Courtines in the town of Millaut in 1587 and Jean Reines and Pierre Seigneuret, together with the proceedings instituted against them by the consuls of the said town of Millaut, shall be annulled and forgotten by reason of this edict, and it shall not be permissible for their widows and heirs, or His Majesty's procurators-general, their substitutes or any other persons, to refer to the matter or to institute an inquiry or proceeidngs, despite the decree given in the chamber of Castres of the tenth day of March last, which will remain null and void, as will all investigations and proceedings made on either side.

56. All lawsuits, proceedings, sentences, trials and decrees concerning either the late sieur de La Noue or sieur Odet de La Noue, his son, since the time they were detained and imprisoned in Flanders in May 1580 and November 1584 and throughout their protracted service in His Majesty's wars, shall be quashed and annulled, as will all consequences of these actions. The said de La Noue shall be heard in appeal, and be restored to the state they were in before these trials and decrees; and they shall not be expected to refund the expenses or pay the fines (if they incurred any), nor may anyone bring a plea against them of non-suit or an extinctive prescription during the said period of time.

Drawn up by the King in council at Nantes, the second day of May fifteen hundred and ninety-eight.

Signed: HENRY. And lower down: FORGET. And sealed with the great seal of yellow wax.

ROYAL WARRANT

This day, the third day of April 1598, the King being at Nantes and desirous of showing kindness to his subjects of the so-called reformed religion, and helping them to meet several heavy expenses they have to bear, has commanded and does command that in future, beginning from the first day of the current month, there shall be placed in the hand of M. de Vierse, whom His Majesty has specially commissioned for this purpose, by each successive treasurer of his coffers, an order for the sum of 45,000 crowns (*écus*) to be used for certain secret matters which concern them, and which His Majesty does not wish to be specified or revealed. This same 45,000 crowns chall be charged to the *recettes générales* as follows: Paris, 6,000 crowns; Rouen, 6,000 crowns; Caen, 3,000 crowns; Orleans, 4,000 crowns; Tours, 4,000 crowns; Poitiers, 8,000 crowns; Limoges, 6,000 crowns; Bordeaux, 8,000 crowns. These figures add up to the sum of 45,000 crowns, payable every quarter from the first and main funds from the *recettes générales*; there shall be no reduction or postponement of payment because of a deficit or any other reason. This sum of 45,000 crowns shall be acknowledged by a receipt, which shall be handed to the royal treasurer to serve as receipt, when he gives the said money orders for the sum of 45,000 crowns drawn on the said *généralités* at the beginning of each year. When for the convenience of the above persons they are required to pay part of the said assignments through private established channels, an order shall be given to all chief treasurers and paymasters in France and all collectors of the said *généralités* to do so, by deducting the said orders from the said *trésoriers de l'épargne*; these orders shall then be named by the said sieur de Vierse, to such people as are named by those of the said religion at the beginning of the year, to draw up the income and expenses of the moneys which these orders must bring in; they will be expected to submit to the sieur de Vierse a true statement of account at the end of the year, with an account of the payments made to creditors, so as to inform His Majesty how these funds are being spent; the said sieur de Vierse, and those representing the adherents of the reformed religion, shall not be expected to account for the expenditure in any chamber. His Majesty has commanded all necessary letters and dispatches concerning these matters to be sent to those involved, by virtue of the present warrant, which he has signed with his own hand and had counter-signed by us, councillor in his council of state, and secretary to his commands.

Signed, HENRI. *And lower down,* DE NEUFVILLE.

SECRET ARTICLES

Today, the last day of April 1598, the King is at Nantes and is desirous of giving all the pleasure he can to his subjects of the so-called reformed religion, in response to the demands and requests made by them, concerning matters they judge necessary to them both for their liberty of conscience and the safety of their persons, fortunes and property. And because His Majesty feels certain of their fidelity, and sincere commitment to his service, and for many other considerations which are important to the welfare and peace of this state; His Majesty, in addition to what is contained in the edict he has recently drawn up, and which is to be published to regulate their affairs, has granted and promised them that all the fortified places, towns and châteaux which they held up to the end of last August, in which there will be garrisons, shall, by a statement which His Majesty will draw up and sign, remain in their hands under the authority and allegiance of His Majesty, for the space of eight years, counting from the day the said edict is published. In the case of other towns they hold where there are no garrisons, no change or innovation is proposed. However, His Majesty does not intend the towns and châteaux of Vendôme and Pontorson to be included in the list of fortified places scheduled to remain in the hands of those of the reformed religion. Nor does he wish to include in their number the town, château and citadel of Aubenas, which he wishes to have at his own disposal; if it is held by someone of the said religion it will not establish a precedent that it shall later pass into the hands of another of the same religion, as in the case of other towns they have been allocated. As regards Chauvigny, it will be restored to the bishop of Poitiers, the seigneur of the locality, and the new fortifications made there are to be demolished. For the upkeep of the garrisons to be stationed in these towns, His Majesty has apportioned a sum not to exceed 180,000 crowns not including those in the province of Dauphiné, which will be paid for in addition to the said sum of 180,000 crowns per annum: he solemnly assures them that he will see that they receive good and valid charges drawn on the main funds wherever these garrisons may be quartered. If these money orders are insufficient, and if the garrisons are running short of money, the difference shall be made good from other revenue, and there shall be no other use made of it until the said sum has been entirely paid and receipted. His Majesty has also promised that when he draws up the statement of the said garrisons he will summon to his side some adherents of the said religion, to ask their advice and hear their remonstrances on what is done, so as to arrange things in future to their utmost possible satisfaction. If during the said eight years there is any reason to change this said statement, whether His Majesty decides it is necessary, or whether they request it, he will use the same procedure as was used originally. As regards the garrisons in the Dauphiné, His Majesty will consult the sieur de Lesdiguières when he draws up the statement relating to them. And when the post of governor or captain of these fortified places falls vacant, His Majesty faithfully promises them to fill it only with a man of the reformed religion, and to require an assurance from the colloquy in which he resides, to the effect that he is of that religion and a person of good character. His Majesty will be satisfied if the candidate, on receipt of the warrant announcing his appointment, produces the statement from his local colloquy, before being confirmed in the appointment. The colloquy, on their part, will be expected to give it him at once without long delays; in case of refusal, they are to explain to His Majesty their reasons. When this period of eight years has elapsed, although His Majesty will have discharged his promise with regard to these towns, and they will have to be restored to him, yet he has promised that, if he continues to keep a garrison in these towns after this time has elapsed, or if he leaves a military governor in them, he will not dispossess the man already in the position to replace him with another. He also declares that he intends, during these eight years and afterwards, to satisfy those of the said religion, to see they have a share in the offices, governorships and other honours that he will distribute, and to make a just and equitable distribution, according to personal merit, as is his practice with his Catholic subjects. However, the towns and fortified places which may in the future be placed under their command, other than those they hold at present, need not create a precedent for being given over to those of the said religion. In addition His Majesty has also agreed that the men entrusted by those of the said religion with guarding the magazines, munitions, powder and cannons of these towns, and those who are to guard them in future, shall continue to hold office and be commissioned by the grand master of the artillery and the quartermaster-general. These letters shall be sent free, and shall contain a clear and full statement of the said magazines, munitions, powder and cannons; but these commissions do not confer on the holders any immunities or privileges. However, they are to be employed according to the statement concerning these garrisons, to be paid their wages out of the sums granted by His Majesty in the foregoing for the upkeep of their garrisons and are not to be a separate charge on His Majesty's other finances. Because the members of the said religion have begged His Majesty to condescend to inform them what he has been pleased to arrange for their worship in the town of Metz, and because this was not clearly stated or included in his edict or secret articles, His Majesty declares that he has despatched letters patent setting forth the following: the chapel formerly built in the said town by its inhabitants will be restored to them so that they may remove the fittings or otherwise dispose of them as they see fit; but they will not be allowed to preach there or practise their religion in any way; however, a convenient place will be provided for them within the town precincts where they can hold public worship without the necessity of a special clause in the edict. His Majesty, in spite of the prohibition laid on the practice of the said religion, at court and its entourage, declares that dukes and peers, officers of the Crown, marquises, counts, governors and lieutenants-general, field marshals and captains of His Majesty's guard, or in his entourage, shall not be subjected to enquiries as to what they do at home, provided it is done in the bosom of their family, behind closed doors, and without any loud intoning, or anything which might reveal the public worship of the said religion. If His Majesty stays longer than three days in towns and localities where worship is permitted, it may after this time be resumed as it was before his arrival. His Majesty declares that in view of the present state of his affairs he has not yet been able to include his lands beyond the mountains, Bresse and Barcelona,[5] in the permission he has given for the reformed religion to be practised. However, His Majesty promises that, when these countries come under his allegiance, he will treat his subjects there as regards religion and other matters granted by his edict as he treats his other subjects, despite what is stated in the said edict; they will, however, be maintained in their present situation. His Majesty will allow those of the reformed religion who are to receive the offices of president and councillor created to serve in the chambers created by his edict, to take office without incurring any expenses at all on the first occasion, according to the statement to be presented to His Majesty by the deputies of the Châtellerault assembly; the same shall apply to the deputies to the procurators and advocates-general set up by the same edict in the chamber at Bordeaux. When the said chamber at Bordeaux and that of Toulouse are incorporated to the said Parlements, these deputies shall enter upon their office without paying. His Majesty will also bestow on messire François

---

[5] Barcelonnette, in the Basses-Alpes.

Pitou the office of deputy procurator-general in the Paris Parlement; this office shall be specially revived for him, and after the said Pitou's death the office shall go to one of the reformed religion. When the first two offices of *maîtres des requêtes* in the King's household fall vacant by death, His Majesty will fill them by such persons of the reformed religion as His Majesty shall think suitable and capable of serving him well, for the price of the tax on *parties casuelles*. And there will be an arrangement whereby in each quarter there are two *maîtres des requêtes* responsible for submitting the petitions of those of the said religion. His Majesty also permits ten of those of the said religion assembled in the town of Châtellerault to live together in the town of Saumur to ensure the operation of his edict until the edict be ratified in his court of Parlement in Paris, although by the terms of the edict they are bidden to disperse at once. However, they may not, in the name of the said assembly, make any fresh demands, nor engage in anything but the attention to the operation of the edict, discussions and the preparing the ground for the commissioners to be selected for this purpose. His Majesty has pledged his good faith and has promised to stand by all the foregoing, in this present warrant which he has insisted on signing with his own hand and which he had countersigned by us, his secretaries of state. He wishes this warrant to have the same effect and force as if its contents were included in an edict ratified in his Parlements. Those of the said religion have agreed, in view of the present state of his affairs, and wishing to be of service to him, not to urge him to frame this ordinance in a more authentic form, since they have such faith in His Majesty's promises and goodness that they are certain he will fulfil his obligations towards them. He has therefore commanded all letters and dispatches necessary to the carrying out of the foregoing, to be sent to them immediately.

Signed, HENRI. *And lower down,* FORGET.

Appendix II
The Revocation of the Edict of Nantes*

Edict of the King

*Prohibiting any farther public exercise of the Pretended Reformed Religion [P.R.R.]
in his kingdom. Registered in the Chamber of Vacations, Oct. 22, 1685.*

Louis, by the Grace of God King of France and Navarre: to all present and to
come greeting. King Henry the Great, our grandfather of glorious memory, being
desirous that the peace which he had procured for his subjects after the grievous
losses they had sustained in the course of domestic and foreign wars, should not be
troubled on account of the P. R. R. as had happened in the reigns of the kings his
predecessors, by his Edict granted at Nantes in the month of April 1598, regulated
the procedure to be adopted with regard to those of the said religion and the places
in which they might meet for public worship, established extraordinary judges to ad-
minister justice to them, and, in fine, even provided by particular articles, for whatever could be thought necessary for maintaining the tranquillity of his kingdom and
for diminishing mutual aversion between the members of the two religions, so as to
put himself in a better condition to labour, as he had resolved to do, for the re-union
to the Church of those who had so lightly withdrawn from it. And as the intention
of the king, our grandfather, was frustrated by his sudden death, and as even the
execution of the said Edict was interrupted during the minority of the late king, our
most honoured Lord and Father of glorious memory, by new enterprises on the part
of the said persons of the P. R. R. who gave occasion to their being deprived of divers
advantages accorded to them by the said Edict, Nevertheless the King, our said late
Lord and Father, in the exercise of his usual clemency, granted them yet another
Edict at Nismes [Nîmes] in July 1629, by means of which tranquillity being established anew, the said late king, animated with the same spirit and the same zeal for
religion as the King our said grandfather, had resolved to take advantage of this repose for attempting to put his said pious design into execution, but foreign wars
having supervened soon after, so that the kingdom being seldom tranquil, from 1635
to the truce concluded in 1684, with the powers of Europe, nothing more could be

---

* David Dundas Scott. *The Suppression of the Reformation in France.* London, 1840.

done for the advantage of religion beyond diminishing the number of places for the public exercise of the P. R. R., by interdicting such as were found established to the prejudice of the dispositions made by the edicts, and by the suppression of the *mi-partie* chambers, these having been appointed provisionally only. God having at last permitted that our people should enjoy perfect repose, and that we, no longer occupied in protecting them from our enemies, should be able to profit by this truce, which we have ourselves facilitated, by applying our whole endeavours to the discovery of the means of accomplishing the designs of our said grandfather and father, adopted as these have been by ourselves since our succession to the crown. And now we see with the thankful acknowledgement we justly owe to God, that our endeavours have reached their proposed end, inasmuch as the better and the greater part of our subjects of the said P. R. R. have embraced the Catholic. And inasmuch as by this the execution of the Edict of Nantes and of all that has ever been ordained in favour of the said P. R. R. remains useless, we have determined that we can do nothing better in order wholly to obliterate the memory of the troubles, the confusion, and the evils which the progress of this false religion has caused in this kingdom, and which furnished occasion for the said Edict and to so many previous and subsequent edicts and declarations, than entirely to revoke the said Edict of Nantes, with the particular articles accorded as a sequel to it, and all that has since been done in favour of the said Religion.

I. We give you to wit that for these causes and others us thereto moving, and of our certain knowledge, full power, and royal authority, we have by this present perpetual and irrevocable edict, suppressed and revoked, suppress and revoke, the Edict of our said grandfather, given at Nantes in April 1598, in its whole extent, together with the particular articles agreed upon in the month of May following, and the letters patent expedited upon the same; and the Edict given at Nismes in July 1629; we declare them null and void, together with all concessions made by them as well as by other edicts, declarations, and arrêts, in favour of the said persons of the P. R. R. of whatever nature they may be, the which shall remain in like manner as if they had never been granted, and in consequence we desire and it is our pleasure that all the temples of those of the said P. R. R. situate in our kingdom, countries, territories and lordships under our crown, shall be demolished without delay.

II. We forbid our subjects of the P. R. R. to meet any more for the exercise of the said religion in any place or private house under anv pretext whatever, even of *exercices réels*, or of bailliages, although the said exercises may have been maintained hitherto in virtue of orders of our council.

III. We likewise forbid all noblemen of what condition soever, to have the religious exercises in their houses and feudalities, the whole under penalty, to be exacted of all our said subjects who shall engage in the said exercise, of confiscation of body and goods.

IV. We enjoin all ministers of the said P. R. R. who do not choose to become converts and to embrace the Catholic, Apostolic, and Roman religion, to leave our kingdom and the territories subject to us within fifteen days from the publication of our present Edict, without leave to reside therein beyond that period, or during the said fifteen days, to engage in any preaching, exhortation, or any other function, on pain of being sent to the galleys.

V. We desire that such of the said ministers as shall convert themselves, continue to enjoy during their lives, and their widows after their decease, during their viduity, the same exemptions from taxes, and from giving quarters to soldiers, which they enjoyed during the exercise of their functions as ministers; and, moreover, we shall cause to be paid to the said ministers a life annuity of one third greater amount than they had as ministers, half of which annuity shall be continued to their wives after their death, as long as they shall remain in viduity.

VI. That if any of the said Ministers wish to become Advocates, or to take the degree of Doctor of Laws, it is our will and pleasure that they enjoy dispensation from three years of the studies prescribed by our declarations, and that after having undergone the ordinary examinations, and been found to have the requisite capacity, they be admitted as Doctors, on payment of the half only of the usual dues received on that occasion at each of the universities.

VII. We forbid private schools for the instruction of children of the said P. R. R. and in general all things whatever which can be regarded as a concession of whatever kind in favour of the said religion.

VIII. As for children who may be born of persons of the said P. R. R. we desire that from henceforth they be baptised by the parish priests. We enjoin parents to send them to the churches for that purpose, under penalty of five hundred livres of fine, to be increased as the case shall happen; and thereafter the children shall be brought up in the Catholic, Apostolic, and Roman Religion, which we expressly enjoin the local magistrates to see being done.

IX. And in the exercise of our clemency towards our subjects of the said P. R. R. who have emigrated from our kingdom, lands, and territories subject to us, previous to the publication of our present Edict, it is our will and pleasure that in case of their returning within the period of four months from the day of the said publication, they may, and it shall be lawful for them to re-enter into possession of their property, and to enjoy the same, as if they had all along remained there; on the contrary, that the property of those who during that space of four months shall not have returned into our kingdom, lands, and territories subject to us, and which property they shall have abandoned, shall remain and be confiscated in consequence of our declaration of the 20th of August last.

X. We repeat our most express prohibitions to all our subjects of the said P. R. R. against them, their wives and children, leaving our said kingdom, lands, and territories subject to us, or transporting their goods and effects therefrom under penalty, as respects the men, of being sent to the galleys, and as respects the women, of confiscation of body and goods.

XI. It is our will and intention that the Declarations rendered against the relapsed, shall be executed according to their form and tenor.

XII. As for the rest, liberty is granted to the said persons of the P. R. R. while waiting until it shall please God to enlighten them as well as others, to remain in the cities and places of our kingdom, lands, and territories subject to us, and there to continue their commerce, and to enjoy their possessions, without being subjected to molestation or hindrance, under pretext of the said P. R. R. on condition, as said is, of not engaging in the exercise, or of meeting under pretext of prayers, or of the religious services of the said religion, of whatever nature these may be, under the penalties above mentioned of confiscation of body and goods: Thus do we give in charge to our trusty and well-beloved counsillors, &c. Given at Fontainebleau in the month of October, the year of grace one thousand six hundred and eighty-five, and of our reign the forty-third.

'Signed LOUIS *visa* LE TELLIER,' and further down, 'By the King, COLBERT.' And sealed with the great seal, on green wax, with red and green strings.

Registered, heard, &c. at Paris, in the Chamber of Vacations, the 22nd of October, 1685.

Signed DE LA BAUNE

Appendix III
Letter from Louis Thibou to Gabriel Bontefoy*

Carolina, the 20th September 1683

Gentlemen and dear Friends,

This is the second letter I am writing to you although you have not yet honoured me by one of yours. In this one I shall give you details about this country and its mode of life, and first of all I shall describe to you that it is a wooded country with lovely savannas or plains crossed by fine rivers very full of fish in which anyone who likes can fish and with enough oysters to feed a kingdom. The land is not too difficult to clear; a man who has a mind to work can easily clear an "arpent" (1 1/4 acres) or more in a month. If a man has five or six "arpents" of land under cultivation and if he works only two months in the year and sows corn and peas after having cleared the land he should be able to reap more than 100 bushels of wheat and 50 or 60 bushels of peas. I myself have not more than that under cultivation and have reaped this year as much as I have just mentioned. This climate is temperate, as you would describe that of Languedoc or Italy, a little warmer than Paris—the winters are almost as long, but the frosts are not so severe. In short I assure you it is a fine climate, very temperate and very healthy, where one feels very fit. Everything you can imagine growing in France or in England grows here. Carolina has good earth, nothing barren about it and it only needs to be cultivated. It is a country where there is an abundance of fish in the right season; in fact one makes the pigs drunk by feeding it to them. I have tried growing vines which do wonderfully well—not those of the country, but those of France, Mādeira and the Canaries which have been introduced here. They produce excellent grapes which are sweet, winey and full of juice. There can never be a lack of them since they are nourished by warmth and soft rain; that is why I am sure of producing here better wine than could be produced in Europe. The native vines also produce very good grapes but the pity of it is that they produce

* Reproduced with permission of *The South Caroliniana Library*, Columbia, South Carolina. The identification of Gabriel Bontefoy as Thibou's correspondent is based on Thibou's statement that he was writing to the godfather of his son Gabriel. Gabriel Thibou was baptized 13 January 1678 in London's Threadneedle Street church with Gabriel Bontefoy acting as his godfather. I am grateful to Jon Butler for this information.

too much wood and too heavy a growth of leaf which hinders the fruit from ripening; all the same I have planted several which have done well. If only I had good vine-stock from Champagne, Suresne and Argenteuil I would very quickly do well in this country for wine is very dear and sells at 30 sous a bottle, as it does everywhere else in America. We only need labour and good plants to do a lot in short time. We have good garden-melons and excellent water-melons of which I am sending you some seeds. We have potatoes in abundance which is a good root out of which we make a drink with molasses or dregs of sugar; it is a liqueur which is as good as beer. These potatoes are mighty good to eat cooked in the oven. A bushel of these roots planted in a little square of earth produces 15 or 20. You must realise that a man here who has 2000 crowns can live better than a gentleman with an income of 4000 "livres" can live in France. In fact any man who has a couple of negroes, a ready-made planta-tion, a maid-servant to look after his household, to milk his cows, to look after his pigs, his poultry and his dovecote can live very happily and that is something a man can have in this country at small outlay. If he wishes to hunt or to have an Indian hunt for him there is no lack of venison or game. An Indian will provide a family of 30 with enough game and venison, as much as they can eat, all the year round for 4 crowns. As for fish there is abundance of all kinds and fishing is such good sport that in this country there is no lack of it, just as in London. Victuals are very cheap, beef only 3 sous a pound at the butcher's, fat pork 3 sous and lean only 2. Wheat is worth 24 sous a bushel and peas 36; one gets 100 pounds of potatoes for only 24 sous. The cattle only feed in the woods, on the plains or on the savanna, the bulls, the cows and the rest of the cattle feed themselves perfectly well at no cost whatever; one has only to keep the calves in the house to bring all the cows back every evening—the only trouble they are is to milk them and they give you a calf every year, which is good profit costing no more to feed a lot than a few; you feed them by their thousands in the woods. As for the pigs, they only need to be given a little corn in the evening to make them come back home, the poultry is easy to rear because of the heat—as you see we have no lack of butter or milk, as well as fat capons, hens and fresh eggs. I admit that a man who starts with nothing has a little difficulty for the first two three years, but a man who has something to back him and can afford a couple of farm hands, a maidservant and some cattle can establish himself very well right away and live very happily in this country. Carolina is a good country for anyone who is not lazy; however poor he may be, he can live well provided he is willing to take a little trouble. Carpenters, cobblers, tailors, and other craftsmen necessary for building or clothing easily make a living. I have no doubt that one of our French friends has put this country in a bad light in his letters but if he had really wished to work he could have done as well as I have and would have had a good word to say for Carolina with as much reason as I, for I assure you that when I arrived with my wife and 3 children I was not worth a farthing and my furniture did not consist of very much, whereas now I am beginning to live well. If I had a couple of farmhands and a serving maid I could live like a gentleman, but I must be patient. I hope with God's help the vines will in time bring me all I want. We have 15 or 16 nations of Indians round us who are very friendly and the English get on well with them; the largest number is not more than 500 strong. They bring them a great quantity of deer skins and furs. There are some tigers and wolves here but no more of the latter than there are in France and the moment a tiger or a wolf catches sight of a man it runs away faster than a deer. Although it is said that there are a great number in the woods I have never seen a live one since I came to the country and only one little dead one that an Indian had killed. As for the crocodile which the English call alligator you cannot get within gunshot of them, for the moment they catch sight of you they dive into the water. Anyhow there are only a few little ones at the sources of the rivers and they have never done harm to any one. There are no more snakes than there are in France and they run away when they hear you so that it is difficult to catch and kill them. As for the rattlesnake, of which there has been so much talk in England, you can easily kill it for it does not move more than a tuft of grass; a child could kill one with a switch. It is true that a few people have been bitten by accident, but there is a good remedy for that here and no one has ever died of their bite; all that has been said about this kind of animals is just a lot of fairy tales. My wife and all my family are well, thank God. My poor little Loton (?) died out here but God has given us a son who is called Jacob after the one we lost in England; the captain of a warship was his godfather. Gabriel is well and kisses the hands of his godfather and godmother. I beg you to communicate this letter to Friend Le Nain and to Mr. Poupé and to Mr. de Baze and to my Friend Ardain and to Mr. Valon and to all my acquaintances; give them my regards; I beg you to let me have some news and to convey the enclosed to M. Mariette of Place Maubert, Paris. I believe there are lots of French in England who have taken refuge there on account of the persecutions. If they want to live in peace they need merely come to this country. They can settle in town or in the countryside, on the plantations where they will be able to live in peace. They will not have to pay any taxes here or money for the high roads nor chimney taxes, for nothing of that sort is charged in this country. All you have to pay is one sou per year to the owner of the land for each "arpent"; wood and resin candles cost nothing at all and tallow candles are very cheap. Those who are willing to come to Carolina will discover the truth of what I say; I would advise all the young men who have a trade to come and settle here rather than stay in England. They could bring us some brandy, white and blue linen and bits of cloth for the Indians; all that serves as good currency and is worth half as much again. I beg you to tell the mother of the little boy I brought along that he is well and that I have received the letter she wrote. Adieu, my dear Friend; please tell M. Valon to write to me and M. de Baze and Friend Le Nain, to whom I feel as close as to you, and M. Poupé and my Friend his wife; and tell her that her brother and sister are well; he has made quite 30 pounds of silk this year; he has let some of it go to ruin by not drawing it, through his negligence; please kiss the hands of all our friends, male and female, to whom I feel as towards you.

Your very affectionate servant
Louis Thibou

My dear Friends,

If you receive any letters from Mme Mariette, you will please send them to me by the first ship leaving for this country.

PS. There is good timber here for building houses which are roofed with planks and boards. Others do it with a sort of lime, made out of oyster shells and clayey soil; those who can afford it make bricks; in short everyone builds as he wishes, maybe with planks sawn from cedars or some other kind of wood; there is lots of cedarwood and fine building is done with it. The children do very well here; they are bigger and fatter than in France or in England. My wife and I wish that some of our friends would come and join us here. My plantation is on the river Ashley which is beautiful and full of fish. There is good land to be obtained behind my plantation and it would suffice for a number of families. I beg you to kiss the hands of M. Prieux who would have done better to come out here than to remain in England. M. Varain is making lots of money at his trade. Excellent apples grow here that become as red as wine, some of them being as good as sweet potatoes. I beg you to send me some pips of good pears, such as winter and summer William pears and butter pears, as well as some horseradish seed. Once again I beg you to write to me and to give us news of our relatives, how they are getting on in France under the persecution. Those who want to come to Carolina could not fail to have opportunities because so many ships arrive from England, the Barbadoes, New England, etc., bringing us horses and cattle. The port here is never without ships and the country is becoming a great traffic centre. Some deputies from Scotland came here to look at the country which pleased them very much; they bought two counties, or provinces, and are preparing to bring over 10,000 people to settle them; I have no doubt that a number of others will follow shortly, people arrive every day from all parts to inhabit this country. That will make Carolina powerful and flourishing in a very short time. Adieu, my dear Friend; I wish you a thousand blessings and am your servant

Louis Thibou

French Protestant (Huguenot) Church, Charleston, South Carolina

Index